IMAGES OF WAR

THE AMX 13 LIGHT TANK

IMAGES OF WAR
THE AMX 13 LIGHT TANK

RARE PHOTOGRAPHS FROM WARTIME ARCHIVES

M P ROBINSON, PETER LAU AND GUY GIBEAU

Pen & Sword
MILITARY

First published in Great Britain in 2018 by
PEN & SWORD MILITARY
an imprint of
Pen & Sword Books Ltd,
47 Church Street, Barnsley,
South Yorkshire.
S70 2AS

ISBN 978-1-52670-167-1

A CIP catalogue record for this book is available
from the British Library.

Typeset by Mac Style Ltd, Bridlington, East Yorkshire
Printed and bound in India by Replika Press Pvt. Ltd.

Pen & Sword Books Ltd incorporates the imprints of
Pen & Sword Books Limited incorporates the imprints of Atlas, Archaeology, Aviation,
Discovery, Family History, Fiction, History, Maritime, Military, Military Classics,
Politics, Select, Transport, True Crime, Air World, Frontline Publishing, Leo Cooper,
Remember When, Seaforth Publishing, The Praetorian Press,
Wharncliffe Local History, Wharncliffe.

For a complete list of Pen & Sword titles please contact:
PEN & SWORD BOOKS LIMITED
47 Church Street, Barnsley, South Yorkshire, S70 2AS, England.
E-mail: enquiries@pen-and-sword.co.uk
Website: www.pen-and-sword.co.uk

Contents

Acknowledgements and Homage to Guy Gibeau

This is the first single volume history of the AMX13 written in English. Our objective was to prepare a comprehensive survey of a weapon that has served 25 armies in one form or another for nearly 70 years. Our focus on the production versions of the AMX13 was decided early on to keep this project to a manageable size. Further study of the many experimental versions of the AMX13 will hopefully be pursued in future. This project bore fruit thanks to our many helpers. Thierry Guillemain, Jerome Hadacek, Steve Zaloga, Simon Dunstan, Pierre Delattre, Marcel Toulon, Philippe Besson, Jakko Westerbekke, Massimo Fotti, Christoph Zimmerli, Lionel Gonnet, Alain Dépré, Daniel Hecket, Denis Verdier, Jean Ancher, Juan Gillard, Michel Huhardeaux, Dante Cesar and the many other contributors are listed in our photo credits. We thank them all for their kindness.

Many soldiers contributed to this book. Colonel Thomas Seignon, Major Bernard Canonne, Coronel Carlos Antonio Arroyo Alonso, Colonel Olivier Carneau, Master Sergeant Luis Pitarch Carrion, General Jorge Andrade Piedra, Major-General Sir Laurence New, the late Commandant Noel Legros, and Lieutenant-Colonel Dick Taylor amongst many others stand out for the large contributions they made in the researching of this work. We also thank Colonel Marc Clerc, commanding officer of the Groupement Blindé de la Gendarmerie Mobile for his kind help in documenting the GBGM's use of the AMX13. This book was researched from published sources as diverse as the AMX13's order book, in many languages. These sources are listed in the notes section, and many were skillfully identified by Peter Lau with his exceptional attention to detail. Of these, Pierre Touzin's writings and those of the armaments engineers of the DGA's COMHART series were notably useful. Writing with Peter and with Guy was wonderful and I thank them both for their thoroughness and their skillful research. As many will know, Guy left us before our book saw print, and I take this occasion to pay him homage.

Lieutenant-Colonel Guy Gibeau wrote a great deal of this book and it was his fond wish to see it completed. Guy was born the son of a tanker who served in Indochina, Algeria, France and West Germany. Guy grew up on bases around tanks, and he saw his path in life from a young age. Guy began his national service at Nancy with the 26e Régiment d'Infanterie just prior to his 20th birthday. He underwent his junior officers training during the summer of

1973, and was posted to the 19e Groupement de Chasseurs Mécanisée (finishing his national service in March 1974 as an aspirant). The day his national service ended Guy volunteered as a regular officer.

In August 1977 Guy was promoted to lieutenant in the regular army and began his specialization training for the mechanized infantry. He served as an AMX13 platoon commander and as an AMX13 SS11 platoon commander in the 8e Groupement de Chasseurs Mécanisée at Wittlich from September 1978 until July 1982. He was promoted to capitaine in August 1982 and moved to the 150e Régiment d'Infanterie at Verdun as an AMX13 squadron commander. In late 1985 his 2e escadron converted to the AMX30. Guy went on to become the regimental gunnery officer, then the regimental NBC officer and finally the operations officer tasked with maneuver and mobilization planning. After the Cold War ended Guy served at the STAT (Section Technique de l'Armée de Terre) detachment at Bourges until July 1993 in command of the infantry weapons test section. Guy was promoted during this period to Commandant. Subsequent assignment back to the 19e Groupement de Chasseurs from August 1993 to July 1996 was followed by staff postings in Germany and France. Guy's promotion to lieutenant-colonel in April 1997 was followed by 13 years of service in the administration of the Région Terre Nord-Ouest military district. Guy and his wife Brigitte had 5 children, and that family was Guy's pride and joy. As we finished this book Guy succumbed after a seven-year battle. Guy's knowledge of the AMX13's long service in the French Army, and of the regiments it served in are evident throughout this book. For Peter and I, it was an honour to have written AMX13 with Guy; to have known him, and above all – to have been his friend. He is sorely missed, and we dedicate this book to him.

Introduction

The AMX13's origins lie in the aftermath of the Second World War. This diminutive tank was designed against the backdrop of French ambitions of national resurgence and entered production in a period when France was dependent on American aid. Commonly described as a light tank, the AMX13 was designed as a turreted tank destroyer. Its design was an ambitious step beyond contemporary practice and away from dependence on American technology. The AMX13 programme concentrated a large industrial group under national direction. It was quickly marketed towards export customers within and outside NATO, and it became the base for a vast list of variants – nearly all of which still serve today.

Chapter One

Origins

France finished the war completely dependent on the goodwill of the United States for its military matériel. The Free French Army armoured force was equipped along American lines in 1944–45, and it fought the Western European campaign organised into US style armoured divisions. American aid under the Marshall Plan and the Mutual Defense Assistance Act (MDAA) financed the reconstruction of France's strategic industries between 1948 and the late 1950s. Against the backdrop of rebellion in the French colonies the Americans agreed in 1948 to help rebuild the French economy and armed forces. A significant caveat existed in that agreement – that American supplied goods and weapons could not be used to fight the Vietminh in Indochina. On 4 April 1949 the North Atlantic Treaty was signed; NATO was created and the U.S. Congress extended the MDAA as part of the larger aim of rebuilding Western European allies to contain communism. The revised American position was timely as France could no longer afford the war against the Vietminh. American aid included the transfer of manufacturing technology and equipment allowing the French defence industry to implement modern efficient manufacturing methods. Lastly the MDAA incorporated the system of offshore orders enabling American funds to be spent procuring weapons sourced from allied nations. Export markets for both the British and French defence sectors were created allowing countries friendly to America to purchase modern weapons such as the Centurion and the AMX13. The French Army in Indochina became dependent on America for military supplies until its eventual defeat. Thus America enabled France to rebuild its postwar army and continue trying to hold its colonies until the early 1960s.[1]

An M4A1E8 76mm gunned Sherman in French service seen in the early 1950s. French dependence on American aid in the 1950s was essential to allow France to resume its place as a major European power. Early MDAP weapons deliveries included a large number of late model Sherman tanks, which served into the early 1960s. (*MP Robinson collection*)

The M26 was also provided to the French pending the arrival of the M47 Patton. This example was photographed in Koblenz in 1954. (*MP Robinson collection*)

The M3A3 and M5 Stuarts served in the French Army for a decade after the war ended, either as training or reconnaissance vehicles in Europe or as a battle tank in the colonial empire. *(MP Robinson collection)*

The infrastructure of roads and bridges in places like Indochina were often inadequate to support even light AFVs. The Stuart series were hopelessly outclassed in terms of armament by 1945, but continued in use until the M24 became available to replace it. *(MP Robinson collection)*

The M24 was used in large numbers by the French, but was too heavy for air transport. This example was widely used in the Algerian campaign. *(MP Robinson collection)*

The M47 replaced the M26 and M4A1E8, and became the principal battle tank in the *Arme Blindée Cavalerie* as a result of the American Military Aid Plan. The first of over 800 M47s were received in 1954, and they served for 20 years until replaced by the AMX30B between 1967 and 1974. (*Thomas Seignon*)

Chapter Two

Design, Funding and Production

The government organ that centralised and directed the French defence industry in the immediate postwar period was DEFA (*Direction des Etudes et Fabrications d'Armements*) – a bureau which had existed since 1936. DEFA's growing importance after the war was symptomatic of the French government's conviction that weapons production and research had to be planned and executed by the state. DEFA had no illusion that heavy weapons production in France in the early postwar years was impossible without American aid. French

The AMX13 prototype demonstrated at Aberdeen Proving Ground in November 1950. The tests were of tremendous importance to DEFA and many of their senior officials attended the trials. A long list of deficiencies was listed by the US report on the AMX13 trials, but the Americans regarded the design as very promising and it went into production with US funding. (*Peter Lau collection*)

One of the AMX13 prototypes was preserved on a plinth at Satory for some years next to the test track. It was photographed here in the mid-1960s and its subsequent fate is not known. (*Bernard Canonne*)

This incomplete AMX13 prototype was exhibited outdoors at the *Museé Des Blindés* in 1984. It could well be the missing Satory exhibit as the Saumur museum is a well-known centre for historic AFV preservation in France. The turret of the prototype is different from the series turret in having a protruding tube for the gunner's sighting telescope and a bulging 'cheek' along the upper edge of the *corps pivotant*. (*Trevor Larkum*)

state arsenals and heavy engineering firms lay in ruins after the liberation and attempts to produce armoured vehicles met with tremendous difficulties.

The best known of the engineers involved with DEFA's efforts to restore French armoured fighting vehicle manufacturing after the war were DEFA director *Ingénieur Général de l'Armement* Étienne Roland and his subordinate *Ingénieur Général de l'Armement* Joseph Molinié. The AMX13 development programme reached its definitive stages under Roland's direction and became the responsibility of Molinié thereafter. Molinié came to be regarded as the father of French tank design in the postwar era, but he represented a large cohort of gifted DEFA armaments designers and engineers. DEFA's technocratic approach to a state controlled armaments agency must have seemed hopeful after the humiliation of occupation and the destruction of France's once vast arms industry.[2]

Molinié began his career as an armoured vehicle designer in the middle of the 1930s at the *Atelier d'Issy les Moulineaux* (AMX) design bureau. During the war he travelled to the United States to study American production and design methods. In 1946 the AMX bureau at Satory resumed tank design under Molinié's direction. At the same time the airborne force's General Demetz (a former cavalryman) was put in charge of a study group responsible for the army's future light tank project. France needed to hold its colonies in order to maintain itself as a world power. Demetz convinced the general staff that an air portable tank destroyer was the ideal weapon for rapid deployment to enable paratroops to hold overseas territories. By early 1947 a follow-on design study was assigned to AMX. The 12 tonne vehicle they envisioned was a strategically mobile (using heavy lift transport aircraft) turreted AFV with a high velocity 75mm main armament. Wartime air-portable tanks had been feebly armed and the existing M-24 Chaffee was too heavy, but AMX addressed the practical problems of a heavily armed air portable tank.[3]

A rare shot of an AMX13 Mle 51 from the first production batch. This photo, taken at Epernay in the latter part of 1952 shows the first AMX13 delivered to the base which was then shared by the *8e Régiment de Hussards* and the *8e Batallion de Chasseurs à Pied. (Thomas Seignon)*

A series 1 tank (French *immatriculation* 826 006) was loaned to Sweden for trials in parallel with negotiations for a possible order of up to 400 tanks. The winter tests in Jämtland revealed that snow scrapers were needed for the idler wheels to prevent the compaction of accumulated snow leading to the breakage of the idler mount. (*SPHF/ Swedish Armour Historical Society/ Kjell Svensson*)

The trial vehicle was given Swedish markings sometime during the loan period. The picture shows a number of interesting features such as the driver's removable windshield, the early hinged driver hatch and the running gear configuration typical for series 1 vehicles. It should be noted that the idler wheels used in Sweden were of a special type for snowy conditions. (*SPHF/ Swedish Armour Historical Society/ Kjell Svensson*)

The Swedish test personnel posing with the trial vehicle. The photo shows that the early FL 10 turret lacked the smoke grenade launchers, the various grab handles as well as the lugs for the lifting of turret. (*SPHF/ Swedish Armour Historical Society/ Kjell Svensson*)

An AMX13 Mle 51 Series 1 disembarking from a landing craft during trials in the early 1950s. This vehicle's hull has many hallmarks of the earliest production AMX13s: the reinforced 6 spoked idler, the pierced muffler cover, headlamps without track guards and the relatively uncluttered glacis. (*Thomas Seignon*)

The urgency of creating heavily armed airborne divisions led the army to extend the tender for alternate designs of a 12 tonne tank chassis in early 1947. AMX, *Forges et Chantiers de la Méditerannée* (FCM) and the Batignolles-Châtillon heavy engineering firm all responded with their own proposals. In May 1948 the *Section Technique de l'Armée* gave a favorable opinion on all three proposals, and each manufacturer produced a prototype chassis. In July 1949 the AMX and FCM designs were evaluated. Batignolles-Châtillon's chassis was not ready in time and was completed in June 1950. The AMX chassis incorporated a simple torsion bar suspension with support rollers, whereas the FCM chassis was equipped with a hydro-pneumatic suspension. Concerns over the complexity of the FCM suspension resulted in the choice of the AMX chassis for production.

Until late 1949 the AMX design was known as the *Char de 12 Tonnes*, *Char Aéroportable de 12 Tonnes* or simply the *AMX12*. The first 5 prototypes were constructed at the AMX workshops. The requirement for air portability soon evaporated as the financial realities of the postwar French defence budgets set in. France could not afford a massive airborne corps or huge transport aircraft to carry tanks. The AMX prototypes continued, however, to be tested until the end of the 1950s with different cargo aircraft to determine air-transportability. The NC211 *Cormorant* and Breguet *Deux-Ponts* transport aircraft were cancelled before development of the AMX design was complete. The AMX programme assumed a new purpose as a light tank intended to replace obsolescent foreign designs. The official designation adopted described the tank by its weight and armament as the *Char de 13 tonnes 75 modèle 51 (AMX)*.[4]

The AMX hull included a front mounted 250HP 8 cylinder Mathis water-cooled petrol engine and a torsion bar suspension with five road wheels on each side. The transmission and final drives were mounted in the front of the hull. The engine occupied the front right of the hull and the driver sat to its left. The rear of the hull housed fighting compartment and turret ring, with the fuel tanks just fore of the rear hull wall. The chassis was the ideal basis for a range of variants. When Mathis became insolvent the engine design rights were purchased by Mecamat and were subsequently bought by SOFAM (*Société Francaise d'Armements et de Motorisation*). The production engine was produced at the Arsenal de Limoges under SOFAM's direction.[5]

The gun adopted for the AMX13 Mle 51 was the *Canon de 75 S.A. Mle 50* (usually shortened to Cn 75 Mle 50 or CN 75-50). This French design employing a shortened version of the barrel of the wartime German 75mm KwK 42 L-70 gun with a new chamber and breech. The weapon had a muzzle velocity of 1000 m/s, an effective range of 1100 metres and could penetrate 175mm of armour at 1000m. It could fire armour piercing and high explosive rounds. This weapon was perfected at the Atelier de Bourges under the direction of *Ingénieur Général* Maurice Carougeau. Over 2600 of the CN 75-50 guns were manufactured by the late 1950s. The coaxial armament was the venerable 7.5mm MAC31 machine gun fed with 150 round drums, a reliable weapon of prewar vintage. The CN 75-50 gun was also designed to fit the M4 Sherman turret with minimum modification. This option was undertaken for Israeli orders in 1954–1955.[6]

The Fives Lille (FL) engineering company was contracted to design the AMX13's turret while the hull was designed by AMX. The basic turret evolved between 1947 and 1949 before the FL10 design was adopted for production. The FL turrets employed an innovative approach to mounting the CN 75-50 gun on a light armoured vehicle hull. Fives-Lille extensively modified its 2 man turrets through the prototype testing phase before standardising two types of 75mm gun turrets by 1950. These were the high velocity 75mm armed FL10 turret with automatic loading, and a simpler medium velocity 75mm gunned FL11 turret with manual loading. Because FL lacked the manufacturing capacity the turret's components were contracted to Schneider and Batignolles-Châtillon.

The FL10 turret selected for the Mle 51 was designed in two parts. In working towards resolving the firepower versus space/weight issue, its designer Michaux was inspired by the operation of an oscillating cement mixer. Michaux's design placed the armament on a vertical pivot on two horizontal trunnions mounted on the armoured steel cradle bridging the turret ring. The upper section (known as the *corps oscillant*) was a hydraulically elevated assembly incorporating the gun mounting, the turret-roof and turret bustle. It fixed the gun breech in line with an automatic loading system carried in the turret bustle.

The lower cradle (*corps pivotant*) served both to traverse and as the trunnions necessary for the upper assembly to elevate and depress. The automatic loader included two rotary magazines of six rounds each (loaded through the turret roof). The turret housed the commander and the gunner, seated on either side of the breech. While the lower cradle section was a solid casting with components welded or bolted to it, the *corps oscillant* was composed of a frontal mantlet casting welded to the roof and bustle sections, themselves made up of flat welded plates. The turret's armour ranged from 40mm to 10mm and only protected the crew from small arms and artillery splinters. The vehicle's small size and mobility were counted upon for much of the crew's protection. In February 1950, the first trial of the turret-integrated AMX chassis took place.[7]

Loading a complete Mle 51 Series 1 aboard a civilian *Bréguet 761 'deux ponts'* during tests in the early 1950s. A specially designed loading ramp permits the tank to be driven directly into the cargo hold. (*Thomas Seignon*)

The tank has been stripped of as many detachable parts as possible to lighten it for transport. The cupola hatch lid and episcopes have been removed but the vehicle must still weigh over 12 tonnes. (*Thomas Seignon*)

In the cargo hold there was very little clearance between the Mle 51 and the fuselage walls as the driver's tense expression implies. (*Thomas Seignon*)

This is the same *Bréguet 761* and the same tank being tested directly from an M19's Rogers trailer into the cargo hold. (*Thomas Seignon*)

Construction of 12 prototype hulls quickly proceeded at AMX and trials of both hulls and complete turreted tank prototypes were conducted through the rest of the year. The French army adopted the AMX design as the *Char 13t-75 Modèle 51* and, in order to secure American funding for series production, AMX13 Prototype 2 was sent to the United States. IGA Roland was among the French delegation that accompanied the prototypes to Aberdeen Proving Ground; it wrote:

> Roland was part of a mission to the USA from 11 February until 10 March 1949 and he made note of the interest shown by his hosts in the originality of the 12-tonne light tank design. At the end of 1949 the French *Secrétaire d'État aux Forces Armées-Terre*, Max Lejeune, asked DEFA to build 4 supplementary prototypes for expected US evaluation. After the selection of the AMX chassis design following the *Section Technique de l'Armée*'s comparative analysis, DEFA obtained the necessary funding very quickly. The Minister for Defence, René Pleven, confirmed interest in trials in the United States in September 1950. The prototype was loaded aboard the *Liberté* at the port of Le Havre on 18 October 1950. Ingénieur Général Roland accompanied the prototype, returning 22 December 1950. (Author's translation.)[8]

Approximately 300 officers and engineers from France, the United States and other countries observed the tests and demonstrations successfully between October and December 1950. The United States agreed to fund the AMX13, but refused to fund the heavier AMX50 that accompanied it and did not fund the proposed AMX13 variants envisioned for the French Army. The AMX13's production group quickly moved the design into production through a conglomeration of three state owned arsenals and four major private industrial concerns. The production group operated under DEFA's direction and included the hull design parent AMX. The turret was built in component form and as complete units within the production group.

The CN 75-50 guns were all manufactured at the Atelier de Bourges. Components like the turret traverse and gun controls were built by SAMM in incrementally improved form during the production run. The early Series 1 production vehicles had numerous teething problems and production was slow as improvements were made and vehicles were re-worked. The slow production of the Series 1 explains why production of the definitive Series 2 (and large-scale French re-equipment with the AMX13 Mle 51) took until 1955 to implement.[9]

The *Atelier de Roanne* (ARE) and three private firms were tasked with producing complete AMX13 hulls on their lines. The *Forges et Chantiers de la Méditerannée (FCM)* plant at La Seyne, Batignolles-Châtillon (BC), and Schneider all received substantial orders. Batignolles-Chatillon and Schneider built FL10 turrets under licence from Fives Lille for hulls assembled at ARE and FCM. Production expanded and the new Schneider plant in Chalon-sur-Saone known by the acronym of SFAC (*Société des Forges et Ateliers du Creusot*) was tasked with assembling AMX13 hulls and components for domestic and export orders. At the end of the 1950s Mle 51 production dropped down to 2 private production lines at the FCM and SFAC facilities while the *Atelier de Roanne* produced components and variants.

From the earliest production batches of 1952 the sales of the Mle 51 for export were arranged by the SOFMA (*Société Française de Matériels d'Armement*) state arms agency. Production of AMX13 vehicles ceased at FCM in 1964 and at ARE in 1967, but ARE continued as an important rebuilding centre for as long as the French army employed the AMX13. Production continued after 1967 for French orders and for export at SFAC. In 1970 SFAC became Creusot Loire Industries and in 1972 Creusot Loire was given responsibility for all AMX13 production which continued on a limited basis for foreign orders until 1987.[10]

Chapter Three

AMX13 Mle 51 Production Series

After the prototypes were evaluated, 135 Mle 51 tanks (known as the Mle 51 Series 1) were ordered in 1950 for troop testing. American funding terms required that production started by specific deadlines, and as a consequence the Series 1 order had to begin production immediately. As a result the Mle 51 design evolved during the slow construction of this first series. On 14 July 1951 the first 10 Series 1 vehicles available participated in the Bastille Day parade. The second 23 were completed during the first half of 1952. They were assigned to the *8ᵉ Régiment de Hussards* and the *Section Technique de l'Armée* for troop testing. The rest of the order was manufactured on the 3 different production lines to provide manufacturing experience, and to build up a stock of vehicles to permit the equipment of the first French Army regiments. Some were also diverted to permit the first export delivery batch to Switzerland. Several minor improvements were made during production. A much larger second series of Mle 1951s was ordered after the order for the Series 1 chassis vehicles was completed. These were produced in 4 incrementally improved chassis sub-types. Over 1,200 Mle 51s were built for French orders roughly between 1952 and 1962; these were classified by chassis types standardised between 1952 and 1958.

Type 2A Chassis: The 2A chassis was the configuration adopted for the definitive AMX13 Mle 51 in 1952. In comparison to the Series 1 chassis it introduced a swivelling driver's hatch, a new sprocket ring carrier and idler wheels with circular holes. It could be distinguished from the later chassis types by five external features: two headlights (originally without guards), a siren on the left fender, four rear lights, a closed exhaust guard with ventilation louvers, and sloping lateral stowage boxes on the track guards.

Type 2B Chassis: The 2B chassis followed with major changes to the electrical system and other minor improvements. The electrical system was changed significantly by the elimination of the blackout lamps in the headlights, the addition of the two front side lights, the replacement of the four rear lights by two new lights and the relocation of the siren to the right side of the hull. Changes to the hull included a revised exhaust guard, the adoption of flat-topped lateral stowage boxes, the elimination of the white reflectors on the front fenders, the addition of red cat's eye reflectors at the rear, the modification of the rear camouflage/tarpaulin net rack and the adoption of a new mirror support.

Type 2C Chassis: The 2C chassis incorporated additional improvements to the electrical system and power train. Changes to the power train encompassed modifications to the engine, clutch, fuel and air induction systems, gearbox, front axle and reduction gear box. The electrical system was essentially similar to that of the type 2B apart from changes to the instrument panel and the addition of an oil pressure warning light and some other junction boxes. One notable change was the incorporation of a junction box that permitted the use of both the more rugged 12V headlight bulbs and the existing stock of 24V headlight bulbs (which failed frequently). Externally, the 2C chassis was almost indistinguishable from the 2B chassis except that its gun crutch kept the gun barrel horizontal when engaged. The type 2A, 2B & 2C chassis all had identical torsion bars and the same ride-height.

Type 2D Chassis: The ultimate chassis type adopted for the Mle 51 light tank was standardised around 1958 (as VTT M56 armoured personnel carrier production started). It began to be delivered on AMX13 Mle 51s built for France and for export from around 1960. The chassis incorporated four return rollers per side, a new pattern cast idler and two Messier shock absorbers fitted to the first and last road wheel support arms on each side of the hull. The hull rear plate introduced a new type of towing hook common to the VTT Mle 56 and the driver's central episcope received a new hooded guard. Other changes were internal and included modifications and improvements to the engine, the fuel supply system, clutch and cooling and electrical systems. This type of chassis was retained for the AMX13 Mle 58 (although this later variant included a different gun crutch and other detail differences).

The FL10 turret also evolved in detail between the original Series 1 vehicles and through the production of the Series 2 tanks, but the subtler FL10 turret variations are more difficult to identify externally. According to surviving documents, there were five production versions of FL10 turret namely, the A, A1R, B, C and D. Each was subject to sub-designation according to the elevation and traverse equipment fitted. Type A turrets of the early vehicles were distinguishable (as built) externally by the use of L-shaped rubber gaskets for sealing the gap -between the elevating and traversing units of the turret. The rubber seal gasket in later types B, C and D (as well as the retrofitted type A1R) was replaced with a pleated canvas bellows type cover which extended or folded with the elevation and depression of the *corps oscillant.*

This Mle 51 Series 2A chassis, with the early pattern FL10 turret is representative of the type. The Mle 51s built on the Series 2A chassis comprised a very substantial part of the French order although exact production figures have yet to be released. (*Collection MP Robinson*)

These Mle 51s of the *1e Régiment de Dragons* were photographed during their annual review in 1957 at Fontevraud. (*Collection Besson*)

The CIDB seen from the air in the hill country east of Trier in the Sarre region. The complex of training circuits was used to train AFV drivers (wheeled and tracked) and home to an AMX instruction squadron from the mid-1950s until the 1980s. The CIDB became the *Centre de Pilotage et de Tir* (CPT) staffed by the mechanized infantry after 1967 and was taken over in turn by the engineers as the AMX10P and the AMX30B were adopted in the mechanized infantry. (*Thomas Seignon*)

An AMX13 Mle 51 on strength of the training squadron at the CIDB photographed during a Remembrance Day parade in the 1950s. (*Thomas Seignon*)

The Mle 51 and M47 training squadrons based at the CIDB photographed during a *prise d'armes* in the 1950s. The Mle 51s are all early Series 2 vehicles with the Type 2A chassis and early pattern FL10 turrets. Prior to 1959 the organization of the French armoured force was slowly evolving from the wartime combat command based armoured division towards a more modern form. This metamorphosis included some bold tactical experiments, like the DMR of 1954-57. The resulting Division 1959 was the first step towards an armoured force configured for fighting on a nuclear battlefield. (*Thomas Seignon*)

The tank garages of the FFA's AMX13 training squadron photographed during the early 1960s before the CIDB (*Centre d'Instruction de Division Blindée*) at Trier was handed over to the mechanized infantry. The photo shows Mle 51s and an early VTT Mle 56 equipped with the CAFL 38 machine-gun turret. Driving both the VTT Mle 56 and the Mle 51 was very similar but without the long barrel of the CN 75-50 gun the VTT was easier to drive. (*Thomas Seignon*)

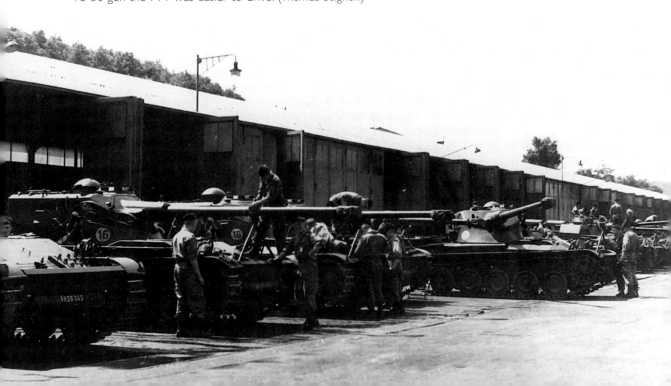

Chapter Four

Rebuilds and Updates

In addition to the two main Mle 51 production series, comprehensive chassis upgrades were made to the French AMX13 park. From the later 1950s some of the Series 1 tanks underwent chassis upgrade modifications to conform to the Series 2B chassis and were re-designated Series 1R (*Séries 1 Rénovée*). These vehicles kept their original sloped tool bins and 12 Volt electrical systems but by 1960 most surviving Series 1 vehicles were converted to AMX-U.S. (AMX13 with Chaffee turret) configuration. The second major chassis rework programme applied to the original AMX13 Mle 51 was the *remise à hauteur* 2R applied from around 1964 to 2A, 2B, and 2C chassis to updated their configuration to approach the definitive Type 2D chassis as far as possible. It is noteworthy that not all Type 2D chassis features could be applied to the earlier vehicles because of fundamental differences in suspension arrangement and availability of spare parts at the point of rebuild.

The suspension was one of the main focus points of the upgrade to 2R standard and new road wheels and tracks were fitted. Theoretically therefore, a type 1R chassis subjected to the 2R retrofit became a Type 1R-2R chassis. A 2C chassis that underwent the 2R work would become 2C-2R, and so on. These rebuild programmes took place at several facilities including the Arsenal de Roanne, the Gien workshops and in divisional workshops. Evidence of comprehensive turret renovation programmes in the same period is very scarce. For the most part the main changes applied to the turrets concerned the provision of new bellows type seals for the junctions of the *corps oscillant* and *the corps pivotant*. The modifications typical of the 2R programme also became standard for the AMX-U.S., AMX13 SS11 and AMX13 C90 conversion programmes that were applied concurrently on the vast majority of French Mle 51s between 1960 and 1978.[11]

Feature	Series I	2A	2B	2C	2D
Headlights	No headlight guards	Headlight guards introduced	Eliminated the blackout lights inside the headlights; blackout lights transferred to side lights	Same as 2B	Same as 2B
Front side lights	Nil	Nil	2 with normal & black-out lights in same housing	Same as 2B	Same as 2B
Rear lights	4 rear lights		Replaced by 2 new lights	Same as 2B	Same as 2B
Siren	Left side		Relocated to right side	Same as 2B	Same as 2B
Rear view mirror and siren protector			Replaced by a new rear view mirror support and protector	Same as 2B	Same as 2B
Front white reflector	Present		Eliminated		
Rear red reflector	None		Incorporated		
Central periscope	Hinged periscope aperture cover				Hinged periscope aperture cover changed to fixed protector hood
Gun travelling clutch	Holds gun in slightly elevated position			Modified to hold gun in horizontal position	Same as 2C
Stowage on front chassis slope	Coiled tow cable and sledge hammer on engine access plate, and spare tracks laid width-wise	Sledge hammer on engine access plate, spare road wheel, and spare tracks laid longitudinally			
Cover of lateral stowage trunks	Inclined			Horizontal	

Feature	Series I	2A	2B	2C	2D
Sheet metal exhaust muffler protector	Muffler fully enclosed under protector with ventilation via punched louvres.		Protector is perforated at the side, exposing the muffler		
Camouflage net support			Modified	Same as 2B	Same as 2B
Tow pintle hitch	Design with a horned profile at the bottom of the hook				Improved design
Sprocket	Same as prototype (early), production standard (late)	Production standard			
Number of support rollers	2				4
Shock absorber (first and last road wheel station)	Telescopic type (Cylindrical)	Telescopic type (Cylindrical)	Same as 2A	Same as 2A	Messier type
Bump stop (of road wheel arms)	Belleville washers (conical-disc springs) type for first road wheel station; rigid metallic stopper for rest of stations				Monobloc rubber with metal backing plate for all road wheel stations
Idler / tension wheel	Un-ribbed wheel with no circular holes (early), Un-ribbed wheel with 6 circular holes (late)	Un-ribbed wheel with 6 circular holes			Wheel with 8 ribs and 8 semi-circular perforations
No. of main gun ammunition	?	37	36	36	36
Rear chassis ammunition rack	Bolted		Welded	Welded	Welded

Chapter Five

The AMX13 Enters Service

The AMX13 Mle 51's entry into widespread service in the early 1950s was delayed by the small number of available vehicles and by the fact that the early 1950s were a period of transition in the *Arme Blindée Cavalerie* (ABC). The new tank was deployed in several types of armoured regiment to determine its ideal tactical application. The most numerous ABC units were the *Régiment de Chars Moyens*, WW2 style medium tank regiments equipped with M4s, or M26s serving in France's armoured divisions. There were also two types of armoured reconnaissance units called *Régiment de Cavalerie Légère Blindée*, (or *Régiment CLB*) which seemed an ideal place to test out the 13-tonner. The *Régiment CLB de Division d'Infanterie* served as organic armour for infantry divisions with 3 squadrons of M26s or M4s. The *Régiment CLB de Division Blindée* was a lighter unit with 3 squadrons of armoured cars serving the reconnaissance role for armoured divisions. The first production Mle 51 Series 1s were tested out in selected CLB regiments in late 1951 and through 1952, where they served in squadron strength as antitank protection for the older tank types or for armoured cars. The first CLB regiment to receive an AMX13 platoon were the *5e Régiment de Hussards,* an M24 equipped unit based in West Germany. On 14 August 1952 the *4e escadron* of the *8e Régiment de Hussards,* then the reconnaissance regiment for the *6e Division Blindée* based at Epernay, took delivery of the second complete squadron. The *Régiment CLB de Division Blindée* was also being re-equipped with EBRs, and it fell to the *8e Régiment de Hussards* to work out tactics and to provide user feedback for the new AMX13 and the EBR simultaneously. The *8e Hussards'* first public presentation of the new tank was the parade down the *Champs Elysées* on 14 July 1953. One of the other aspects of the *8e Hussards'* experience with the AMX13 at Epernay over the following five years was that they received small numbers of the AMX13 FL 11, which served as training vehicles for crews destined to take the type to North Africa.[12]

By all accounts the AMX13 was too loud a vehicle for the liking of the ABC's reconnaissance troops and its 3-man crew was not ideal for reconnaissance tasks. When the *2e Régiment de Hussards* converted two of their squadrons to the AMX13 in 1953, they tested out the tactical possibilities of operating them alongside M26 Pershings in the remaining two squadrons of the regiment. The *13e Régiment de Dragons Parachutistes*, the armoured regiment of the *25e Division d'Infanterie Aéroportée* (25e DIAP) based at Castres also received a squadron of Mle 51 Series 1 in June 1953 that served alongside the M4s and M26s in their other two squadrons. The *11e Régiment de Cuirassiers* (which also operated 2 squadrons of EBRs as a CLB regiment until

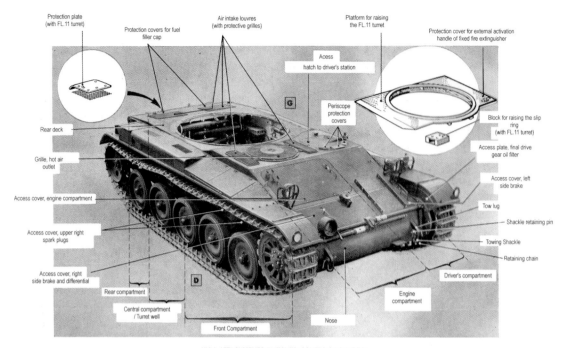

Protection plate
(with FL.11 turret)

Protection covers for fuel
filler cap

Air intake louvres
(with protective grilles)

Platform for raising
the FL.11 turret

Protection cover for external activation
handle of fixed fire extinguisher

Acess
hatch to driver's station

G

Periscope
protection
covers

Block for raising the slip
ring
(with FL.11 turret)

Access plate, final drive
gear oil filter

Access cover, left
side brake

Rear deck

Grille, hot air
outlet

Access cover, engine compartment

Access cover, upper right
spark plugs

Access cover, right
side brake and differential

Tow lug

Shackle retaining pin

Towing Shackle

Retaining chain

Rear compartment

D

Central compartment
/ Turret well

Front Compartment

Nose

Engine
compartment

Driver's compartment

HULL ATTACHMENTS (HATCHES, COVERS & LOUVRES)

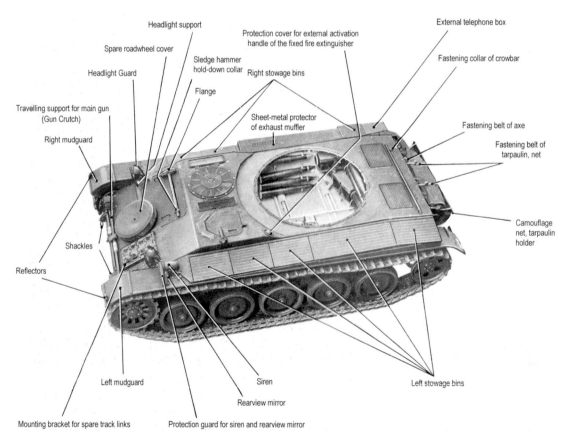

Headlight support

Spare roadwheel cover

Headlight Guard

Travelling support for main gun
(Gun Crutch)

Right mudguard

Shackles

Reflectors

Left mudguard

Mounting bracket for spare track links

Sledge hammer
hold-down collar

Flange

Protection cover for external activation
handle of the fixed fire extinguisher

Right stowage bins

Sheet-metal protector
of exhaust muffler

External telephone box

Fastening collar of crowbar

Fastening belt of axe

Fastening belt of
tarpaulin, net

Camouflage
net, tarpaulin
holder

Left stowage bins

Siren

Rearview mirror

Protection guard for siren and rearview mirror

EXTERNAL ACCESSORIES OF THE HULL

Two views showing the configuration of a typical Type 2A chassis. (*Thomas Seignon*)

1955) and *2e Régiment de Dragons* soon followed converting individual squadrons to the Mle 51 during 1954. The difficulties of operating tanks and armoured cars together in the CBL units resulted in the decision to use the AMX13 in dedicated regiments. The AMX13 Mle 51 was introduced as equipment for complete *Régiments de Chars Légers* (light tank regiments) from 1954 onwards starting with regiments re-equipped in France and in West Germany.[13]

In the period 1954-57 an important formation-level tactical experiment was attempted, which came to be known as the *Brigade Javelot* and subsequently as the *7e Division Mécanisée Rapide*. The experimental organization employed in the division offered French tacticians a radical approach to the problems of combined arms warfare. It was made up of 4 new *Régiment Inter Armes* (RIA) – a combined arms regiment that included armour, artillery and infantry. Only the 7e DMR employed RIAs, which included two AMX13 squadrons and two squadrons of *voltigeurs antichar* mounted in jeeps and halftracks. Artillery was attached as required and each RIA was supposed to function as a self-sufficient tactical entity. Only 3 of 4 planned regiments (the *2e Régiment de Dragons*, the *21e Régiment d'Infanterie Coloniale*, and the *Régiment Colonial de Chasseurs de Chars*) were ever configured as RIAs and the 7e DMR was never completed. The AMX13 with its multiple planned derivatives seemed to be the ideal weapon for the RIAs, but

The *30e Régiment de Dragons* served with AMX13s in North Africa from late 1956 until 1961, first in Morocco and after July 1957 in various parts of Algeria. Its 3 AMX13 squadrons deployed as detached sub-units spread over large areas, responsible for route security, reconnaissance, and engaging armed bands of rebels. The regiment lost 52 officers and men killed during this period (and 59 others were wounded in action). The photo shows preparations for a squadron parade at Montagnac, Algeria, on 11 November 1958 – note the tank crewman's helmet. (*Thomas Seignon*)

The squadron commander's Mle 51 photographed with the squadron pennant carried at the gunner's position. The AMX13's antitank capabilities were ill-used in Algeria, but many AVF types were deployed throughout the conflict. (*Thomas Seignon*)

The parade is followed up by the squadron's ubiquitous Mle 55 *Char de Dépannage*, an absolute necessity for any deployment of the squadron in the field. The 30e RD employed the AMX13 Mle 51 until it left Algeria in 1961 and was then re-equipped with the M47. (*Thomas Seignon*)

A view seen from the air of the *prise d'armes* conducted prior to the Remembrance Day parade. Some Hotchkiss M201s, the licence-built versions of the American Jeep, can be seen. By the time the 30e RD left Algeria in 1961 it had served under no less than 5 different infantry and armoured divisions. (*Thomas Seignon*)

Primarily designed for transport by air this AMX13 was easily lifted aboard a transport vessel for shipment by sea. (*Collection Thomas Seignon*)

In September 1961 the 30e RD's AMX13s were lifted aboard the *Foudre* at Bone for the regiment's voyage back to France. (*Collection Thomas Seignon*)

The AMX13's career in Algeria was not an unqualified success. Besides the *30e Régiment de Dragons*, the *2e Régiment de Dragons*, the *Régiment Colonial de Chasseurs de* Chars and the *21e Régiment d'Infanterie Coloniale*, a few other regiments employed the Mle 51 there as part of their equipment. (*Collection Jerome Hadacek*)

The *9e Régiment de Hussards* and the *2e Régiment de Spahis Algériens* operated the AMX13 in single squadrons as *Régiment Blindés Type AFN*, and the type was also employed for some time by the Foreign Legion Cavalry. (*Collection Jerome Hadacek*)

French Army Mle 51s from the first production series carrying Operation Musketeer identification markings in 1956 (the white H marking on the turret rear was one of the Anglo-French recognition signs employed in hopes of avoiding friendly fire incidents, derived from the original name of the operation to re-occupy the Suez Canal zone – *Operation Hamilcar*). (*Collection Claude Dubarry*)

Mailly was used as a training ground by many units and was also an important part of the cavalry (and later mechanized infantry) officers' training courses conducted through the St Cyr Coetquidan programmes. This Mle 51 Type 2C was photographed during an officers' training course from the Promotion 1958-1960 Maréchal Bugeaud in 1960. (*Collection Besson*)

the division and its novel approach to mobile warfare existed only briefly in Europe as part of the army's general reserve. At Suez in November 1956 two squadrons of the *21e Régiment d'Infanterie Colonial* RIA supported by a squadron of the *8e Régiments de Dragon's* M47s saw action very successfully. Soon however the *7e Division Mécanisée Rapide* became embroiled in the chaos of the war in Algeria, and it missed the chance it seemingly deserved to prove itself as a template for a new standard armoured division.

After the Foreign Legion's return from Indochina in 1954-55, two squadrons of the *2e Regiment Étranger de Cavalerie* received Mle 51s. The unit was reorganized to serve a similar function to the *Régiment CLB* and the AMX13 squadrons were immediately trained for service in Morocco. The *2e REC* included a headquarters squadron, a reconnaissance squadron (*1e Escadron*) and two squadrons of AMX13s (*2e Escadron* and *3e Escadron*). The two AMX13 squadrons served in Morocco until March 1956. In May and June 1956 the regiment's AMX13s were sent to support the Legion units operating in Algeria. In August 1956 the *2e Escadron* was attached to the *1e Régiment Étranger Parachutiste*, moving with the *10e Division Parachutiste* in November to take part in Operation 'Musketeer'. The rest of the *2e REC* moved to Algeria in October 1956 and both AMX13 squadrons served in the Suez operation. The 1e REP was involved in the successful amphibious operation at Port Said but after the ceasefire the 1e REP returned to Algeria in December. The 1e REP briefly retained the *2e Escadron* for operations in Algeria but the regiment amalgamated with the newly raised *1er REC* in 1957 and re-equipped with EBRs.[14]

The length of the CN-75-50's barrel in relation to the hull is quite evident with the turret traversed to the 3 o'clock position. In steep terrain it was imperative for the driver to be aware of which way the gun was pointing! The chalky Champagne soil in the training area produced glutinous mud in wet weather and in dry weather thick dust inevitably coated all and sundry. (*Collection Besson*)

A Mle 51 of the 11e RCh in Berlin in the early 1960s. (*Collection J.J. Montegnies*)

The *11e Régiment de Chasseurs à Cheval* (11e RCh), a French cavalry regiment, was stationed in West Berlin for many years. It employed the AMX13 for nearly 3 decades. *Armagnac*, an Mle 51 with a type 2B or 2C hull was photographed in 1962. The turret seal bellows is visible beneath the turret bustle as are the rear tarpaulin rack and the original pattern idler. (*Juan Gillard*)

A low angle shot of *Alsace* of the 11e RCh during preparations for an official parade in 1962 (very likely rehearsing for the Allied Forces Day parade or for the *14 Juillet* parade). This is an early Mle 51 built on the Series 2A chassis with an early FL10 turret. The glacis stowage was typical – as were the cat's eye reflectors and the slanted tool bins which are not clearly visible from this angle. (*Juan Gillard*)

A line of AMX13 Mle 51s of the 11e RCh in 1962 during rehearsals for a parade. 2A hulls are visible on all but the closest vehicle which is built on the Type 2B or 2C chassis. The second tank is very likely named *Eckmuhl*. (*Juan Gillard*)

Some turret features can be recognised amongst the crowded lines of 11e RCH AMX13 Mle 51s photographed in the *Quartier Napoléon* in West Berlin in the summer of 1962. Two different types of turret joint seals *(the French term for the later bellow type seal was 'soufflet' while the earlier one was 'couvre-joint')* are fitted, typical for AMX13 units at the time. Like most AMX13 regiments a mixture of different Mle 51 series were on strength with the 11e RCh. (*Juan Gillard*)

The 1962 *14 Juillet* parade of the 11e RCh in West Berlin. *Alsace* (which was depicted on page 32) is in the foreground. A similar vehicle is in the background to the right while to the left a slightly later production vehicle with the type 2B or 2C chassis is partly visible. (*Juan Gillard*)

An early Mle 51 with early pattern FL10 turret and Type 2A chassis, and a later Mle 51 with Type 2B or 2C hull and later pattern FL10 turret pass the reviewing base. The earlier vehicle has been modified with the *triangle de securité* behind the driver's hatch. The later vehicle is named *Smolensk*. (*Juan Gillard*)

This early Mle 51 of the 11e RCh is seen crossing a bridge during field manoeuvres in the early 1960s. It is either a Series 1R or an early Series 2A hulled vehicle and has an FL10A turret. (*Juan Gillard*)

The early Mle 51 built on the Type 2A chassis featured four rear hull lights as seen on this vehicle of the 11e RCh in 1962. The AMX13 was light enough to cause minimal damage on public roads and was frequently seen on the streets in the French sector of West Berlin. (*Juan Gillard*)

The AMX13 Mle 51 had a good cross country performance for its time. This is an early Mle 51 with the Type 2A chassis and initial pattern FL10 turret of the 11e RCh. Note the early pattern gun travel lock. (*Juan Gillard*)

This illustrates the risk of the gun embedding itself whilst crossing steep terrain. (*Juan Gillard*)

Muddy terrain was hard on the crew, especially the driver. (*Juan Gillard*)

Alsace of the 11e RCh crossing a muddy training ground near West Berlin in 1962. *(Juan Gillard)*

The AMX13 was employed throughout the Algerian war. It was deployed with the *2e Régiment de Dragons* and the *30ᵉ Régiment de Dragons* to permit the French army to confront the FLN and any possible foreign (Egyptian) intervention supporting it. The Mle 51 also saw more limited use in a few cavalry regiments as partial equipment. The *Régiment Blindé Type Afrique du Nord (AFN)* had a unique organisation with only a fraction as many tanks as a metropolitan armoured regiment. In Algeria armoured regiments that retained their armour for the campaign employed a mixture of AFVs; generally including a squadron mounted in halftracks, another in M8 armoured cars, and only one in tanks (most often M24s). The AMX13 Mle 51 was not an ideal vehicle to support infantry against guerillas but it was employed with some success in Algeria due to its excellent mobility. The main threats were landmines and bazooka type weapons against which the AMX13 Mle 51 proved very vulnerable due to its thin armour. The bulk of the Mle 51 fleet was held in France and West Germany, and by the late stages of the conflict the AMX-U.S. made up the bulk of the AMX13s deployed in Algeria.[15]

As the ABC rationalized its unit structures and equipment in the second half of the 1950s, the AMX13 became an important symbol of the army's modernization. The AMX13 Mle 51 ended up serving in conventional armoured divisions in *Régiment de Chars de 13 Tonnes* (standardized by about 1957 with 3 squadrons of 17 tanks and 3 tanks at regimental headquarters). The medium tank regiments re-equipped with the M47 followed a similar structure. The experiments of the mid-1950s were forgotten and the army focused on its NATO commitments.

Chapter Six

The AMX13 FL-11 and AMX-U.S.

When first ordered, the Mle 51 could not be used without regard for American sensibilities in France's overseas empire (for example in Indochina). On 16 Feb 1952, the Minister for Indochina requested AMX13 tanks be sent to serve in the French cavalry units fighting the Vietminh because the M24 and M5A1 were too heavy or too poorly armed to suit local conditions. Because the Mle 51's armament was unsuited for guerilla warfare it was decided to equip the AMX13 with the compatible FL11 turret in production for the EBR armoured car, and AMX received an order in February 1954 to build 5 vehicles (with one vehicle to be built immediately). An airlift test followed in March, which proved that the tank still needed to be disassembled into 3 loads in order to be carried by the *Armée de l'Air*'s existing heavy transport aircraft. The rest of the original order was built in May and troop testing commenced while a further 15 vehicles were ordered.

The FL11 turret was manufactured in the EBR production group by the *Société des Ateliers de Construction du Nord de la France* (SACNF) and by the *Société Alsacienne de Constructions Mécaniques* (SACM). The FL11 was considered ideal to make the AMX13 suitable for deployment in Indochina. The AMX13 FL11s were built on Series 2A chassis and they weighed 1.5 tons less than the standard Mle 51; the Indochina war was, however, over before any were dispatched. They were eventually tested in North Africa where the M24 was already in widespread use. Production never ensued because the need for the AMX13 FL11 had evaporated. Most surviving AMX13 FL11s were handed over to the fledgling Moroccan army in 1956 and very little information has survived concerning the vehicle's subsequent career.[16]

The army and DEFA also examined and proved ways to use the FL10 turret on existing M24 hulls as a cheap way to modernise the French Chaffee fleet in 1956, but the concept was never pursued. The inverse, mounting the M24 turret on the AMX13 hull, made more sense because the FL10's automatic loader and the sensitive fusing on the CN-75-50's high-explosive rounds proved a dangerous combination. High explosive rounds had to be manually loaded into the Mle 51's breech by the commander when required (an awkward task). Fitting the M24's turret to the AMX hull required an adaptor (because of the Chaffee's tall turret basket) but otherwise proved a simple conversion. Trials were successfully conducted from December 1959 to January 1960 and 150 conversions were ordered in March 1960. The conversion of reconditioned vehicles to mount the M24 turret on many early production vehicles (with Type 1R chassis but also on some Type 2A, 2B and 2C chassis) was conducted at Gien. These

The AMX13 FL-11 was conceived based on a 1953 ministerial request to send AMX13s to Indochina. The need evaporated once the Indochina war ended and they were sent to North Africa instead. This photo shows an AMX13 FL-11 with a Type 1R chassis. (*AMX/Peter Lau Collection*)

This following sequence of photos taken in the early 1950s illustrates some of the challenges of air transport, using a Bristol 170 Freighter, that were tested out during the prototype trialling of the AMX13. The AMX13 was broken down into 3 separate loads; that seen here includes the tracks and FL11 turret packed on a pallet sized to fit a GMC truck's cargo bed. The FL11 turret was standard for the EBR but could be mounted on the lighter Mle 51 and as, shown here, it was considered for this reason from the prototype stage. Only a very few AMX13 FL11s were produced in 1952 and 1954. (*Thomas Seignon*)

The second load included elements of the suspension. (*Thomas Seignon*)

The three loads seen here carried by 3 GMC trucks. Given the carrying capacity of the GMCs and the weight of at least 2 of the pallets, the range of the trucks would have been limited. (*Thomas Seignon*)

The hull is loaded through the nose of the Bristol Freighter; note the wooden pilings necessary to obtain the correct loading angle (and to avoid damaging the aircraft). (*Thomas Seignon*)

The hull is anchored solidly in the cargo hold. The load required precise positioning to avoid upsetting the aircraft's trim in flight. (*Thomas Seignon*)

This loading trial, also in the early 1950s, was conducted on a *Nord Noratlas* with the AMX13 broken down into separate loads. (*Thomas Seignon*)

hybrids retained the complete M24 turret armament including the co-axial M1919 .30 Browning and an M2 12.7mm Browning mounted on the turret roof. They served with a 4-man crew, carrying the official designation of AMX-U.S. (but known unofficially to the troops as the "*AMX13 Chaffee*"). They gave satisfactory service in Algeria until the final French withdrawal in 1964. Following the end of their brief service in Algeria, the Chaffee's gun and mantlet were removed and replaced with a plexiglass window to convert some of the remaining AMX-U.S. into driver trainers and none are believed to have served in the AMX13 regiments stationed in France or in West Germany. The disarmed AMX-U.S. served into the 1980s in dwindling numbers and the rest were scrapped or expended as targets.[17]

The AMX-U.S., or AMX Chaffee as it was often known, was an effective improvisation. The turret ring riser employed is clearly visible in this picture of one converted from a Series 1R or Series 2A chassis. The rebuilt chassis received many of the upgrade features seen on later series 2 vehicles and fittings like the gun crutch were removed during the conversion. (*Thomas Seignon*)

Some sources describe the AMX-U.S. as a convenient way to use M24 turrets from worn out Chaffees, but as many were based on Series 1R hulls the inference is that some of the hulls were also from very early production AMX13s. The fate of the original FL10 turrets made redundant by the creation of possibly 150 of these hybrids is unknown – but they may have been rebuilt, turned into training aids or simply sold back to the manufacturers. (*Thomas Seignon*)

The *Escadron Type AFN* was composed of 2 tank platoons of 4 tanks, a support group and a dismounted group in halftracks. The tank platoon, seen here entering an urban area in Algeria late in the conflict, includes 3 AMX13s based on Series 1R or 2A chassis and an M8 75mm GMC. The jeeps carry troopers serving as infantry. (*Thomas Seignon*)

Chapter Seven

The AMX13 Mle 58

By the late 1950s the AMX13 needed to be up-gunned or replaced. The CN 75-50 firing conventional armour piercing ammunition could not defeat the latest Soviet T54 medium tanks frontally, and DEFA was already developing the Obus Gessner (or Obus G) ammunition for the 105mm gun expected to arm the AMX30 medium tank. The Obus G was a hollow charge round incorporating a bearing race to prevent the spin from firing through a rifled barrel degrading its performance.

Obus G rounds were developed in 90mm and 105mm but this costly munition was not considered for 75mm weapons. A second option for DEFA was to develop more powerful 75mm ammunition and studies were conducted at the Atelier de Bourges to develop a 75mm sub-calibre penetrator round (functioning like a British discarding sabot round). Funding shortfalls forced the army to dismiss a wholesale replacement of the AMX13 and delayed the decision on upgrading the Mle 51 until 1963. In the meantime DEFA explored and proved the concept of up-gunning the Mle 51. A modified Mle 51 was tested in 1956 with a 105mm D1504 gun (derived from the CN 105mm F1 under development at Bourges to arm the AMX30). The D1504 gun had a less impressive range than the longer CN 105 F1 that went on to arm the AMX30 due to its lower chamber pressure, smaller powder charge and shorter gun barrel. A double baffle muzzle brake was fitted to permit its use on the AMX13's light chassis. The 105mm gun was standardized by DEFA as the CN-105-57 and the modified FL10 turret received the Fives-Lille designation FL12. The up-gunned AMX13 was built on the Type 2D chassis and was designated AMX13 Mle 58. The CN-105-57 could also be adapted to other mountings including the 76mm gunned Sherman turrets. Both the FL12 turret and the kit for modifying the 76mm Sherman turret were eventually successful on the export market.

The CN-105-57 combined with the FL12's simple fire control system still left the Mle 58 an effective range of only 1000 metres. Attempts to extend the Mle 58's range with a coincidence rangefinder for the FL12 turret at the Atelier de Puteaux (APX) were conducted between 1955 and 1960 without success. The 0.70 metre base width rangefinder was proposed for the tank commander, and was linked to the gunner's sight (which would have been equipped with a trunnion tilt correction device and a movable sight graticule). In such cramped confines as the FL12 turret there was no room for improved fire controls using the technology of the day. Further trials conducted in 1961-1962 by the DGA and EMAT to equip the FL12 with a British style ranging gun were equally unsuccessful. The FL12 already had little room for coaxial machine-gun ammunition, let alone a 12.7mm ranging weapon. The production FL12 turret therefore perpetuated the design principles and limitations of the FL10 turret.

The Mle 58 was the most heavily armed light tank of its day, a 15 tonne vehicle that could knock out almost any contemporary battle tank. The French Army were impressed and evaluated the design at length but orders did not ensue. Production at SFAC for export under SOFMA's direction began in 1960 and continued until the late 1970s. Over 400 of the CN-105-57 guns were manufactured at the Atelier de Bourges for AMX13 Mle 58s ordered during the 1960s and a substantial quantity followed for the Israeli M51 programme, later export Mle 58s and for FL12 turrets ordered for the Austrian SK105. The CN-105-57 represented the limits of what the FL turret design could bear in terms of recoil and bulk. The 105mm gun firing the Obus G at 800 metres per second could penetrate 150mm of armour plate sloped at 60 degrees (or 300mm of vertical armour) regardless of range. The drawback was that accuracy beyond ranges of 1000 metres decreased considerably. Despite the fact that the EMAT and DEFA itself argued in favour of adopting the AMX13 Mle 58, the simultaneous cost of bringing the AMX30 and other new weapons into service had to be borne. The French Army never ordered the Mle 58 which was built entirely for export.[18]

The AMX13 Mle 58 mounted the 105mm CN-105-57 in the FL12 turret. (*Philippe Besson*)

A double baffle muzzle brake was required to minimise recoil. (*Dick Taylor*)

The CN-105-57 fired the Obus-G round, an expensive and sophisticated hollow charge round that incorporated an internal ball race that reduced spin allowing it to be fired through a rifled barrel. The Mle 58's CN-105-57 and AMX30's CN-105-F1 105mm guns were not as effective as the L7 type rifled 105mm guns when firing kinetic energy projectiles. Despite this fact, their antitank performance firing the Obus-G HEAT type projectile was excellent, and with the Obus G armour penetration remained consistent even at maximum range. (*Dick Taylor*)

Besides the new gun and detail changes made to accommodate the larger ammunition, this AMX13 Mle 58 was very similar to the Mle 51 based on the Type 2D chassis produced in the early 1960s. (*Jerome Hadacek*)

Besides a few examples extensively evaluated by the French Army and the DGA, no Mle 58s were ordered by France. (*Jerome Hadacek*)

Chapter Eight

Division 1959

The colonial conflicts of the 1950s were a huge drain on the forces available for French NATO commitments. After the experiment of the DMR ended the army settled on a more conventional armoured division for the 1960s, known as the *Division 1959*. The *Division 1959s* were the French Army's answer to modernizing the 1944 era armoured division structure into formations capable of fighting on a nuclear battlefield. New weapons were adopted for all arms and the old Combat Command based organization was replaced with a large division composed of three brigades. The *Division 1959* could exist in two forms – the armoured division (*Division Blindée*) with 2 armoured brigades and a single mechanized brigade, or the mechanized division (*Division Mécanisée*) with 2 mechanized brigades and a single armoured brigade. There were 2 *Régiments de Chars de Bataille* (equipped with M47s) in the *Brigade Blindée* (armoured brigade), and a *Régiment de Chars Légers* equipped with AMX13 Mle 51s in each *Brigade Mécanisée* (mechanised infantry brigade). Although five of these large divisions were planned, only four were fully constituted and based in both West Germany and in eastern France.

The AMX13 family figured prominently in the *Division 1959*, and the introduction of the AMX13 VTT Mle 56 armoured personnel carrier was a significant new component in its equipment. The *Régiment de Chars de Bataille* equipped with M47 Pattons at first included a squadron of organic infantry in halftracks, which were replaced with VTT Mle 56s in the early 1960s. A mechanised infantry regiment with fifty-six AMX13 VTT Mle 56s in four squadrons served in each armoured brigade as the third regiment. The *Brigade Mécanisée* implemented in 1959-60 was equipped almost completely with AMX13 type vehicles. The division's artillery included field artillery units equipped with OB-105-Au-50 self-propelled guns.

The *Régiment de Chars Légers* (also referred to as *Régiment de 13t* and as *Régiment d'AMX* in official manuals) included an *escadron de commandement et de services* (equivalent to a headquarters squadron) and three AMX13 Mle 51 squadrons (or *Escadron de Chars AMX (75)*). After 1964 an AMX13 SS11 squadron was added to bolster the antitank capabilities of these regiments. Each *Escadron de Chars AMX (75)* included 15 tanks in 3 combat platoons (*pelotons de combat*) of 5 tanks. A command platoon was mounted in jeeps and every combat platoon was provided with a jeep for the commander and with a two jeep *groupe d'orienteurs*, whose job was to reconnoitre fire positions and to establish fire positions with optical rangefinding equipment. The rangefinding teams were an innovative tactical feature that allowed the platoon and squadron commanders to make the most of the CN-75-50's range and to permit the Mle 51s to be used from ambush positions wherever possible.[19]

Division 1959

Brigade	Regiment	material 1	material 2	material 3* (APC)	Field Artillery
1e Division Blindée Trèves (FFA)					
1e Brigade Blindée	1e Régiment de Cuirassiers	54 x M47	12x AMX-13 SS11	12x AMX-13 VTT M56	8e Régiment d'Artillerie de Marine
	6e Régiment de Cuirassiers	54 x M47	12x AMX-13 SS11	12x AMX-13 VTT M56	16x 105mm AU
	2e Groupe de Chasseurs Mécanisé	56x AMX-13 VTT M56			
3e Brigade Blindée	4e Régiment de Cuirassiers	54 x M47	12x AMX-13 SS11	12x AMX-13 VTT M56	16e Régiment d'Artillerie
	5e Régiment de Cuirassiers	54 x M47	12x AMX-13 SS11	12x AMX-13 VTT M56	16x 105mm AU
	8e Groupe de Chasseurs Mécanisé	56x AMX-13 VTT M56			
11e Brigade Mécanisée	6e Régiment de Dragons	54x AMX-13 MI 1951	12x AMX-13 SS11		2e Régiment d'Artillerie
	16e Groupe de Chasseurs Mécanisé	56x AMX-13 VTT M56			16x 105mm AU
total		216x M47, 54x AMX-13 MI 1951, 168x AMX-13 VTT M56	60x AMX-13 SS11		48x 105mm AU
3e Division Mécanisée Fribourg (FFA)					
5e Brigade Blindée	2e Régiment de Cuirassiers	54 x M47	12x AMX-13 SS11	12x AMX-13 VTT M56	24e Régiment d'Artillerie
	12e Régiment de Cuirassiers	54 x M47	12x AMX-13 SS11	12x AMX-13 VTT M56	16x 105mm AU
5e Brigade Mécanisée	24e Groupe de Chasseurs Mécanisé	56x AMX-13 VTT M56			
12e Brigade Mécanisée	43e Régiment Blindé d'Infanterie de Marine	54x AMX-13 MI 1951	12x AMX-13 SS11		11e Régiment d'Artillerie
	19e Groupe de Chasseurs Mécanisé	56x AMX-13 VTT M56			16x 105mm AU
13e Brigade Mécanisée	5e Régiment de Dragons	54x AMX-13 MI 1951	12x AMX-13 SS11		34e Régiment d'Artillerie
	42e Régiment d'Infanterie Mécanisée	56x AMX-13 VTT M56			16x 105mm AU
total		108x M47, 108x AMX-13 MI 1951, 168x AMX-13 VTT M56	48x AMX-13 SS11		48x 105mm AU
7e Division Mécanisée Mulhouse					
7e Brigade Blindée	30e Régiment de Dragons	54 x M47	12x AMX-13 SS11	12x AMX-13 VTT M56	74e Régiment d'Artillerie
	1e Régiment de Dragons	54 x M47	12x AMX-13 SS11	12x AMX-13 VTT M56	16x 105mm AU
	35e Régiment d'Infanterie Mécanisée	56x AMX-13 VTT M56			
6e Brigade Mécanisée	2e Régiment de Dragons	54x AMX-13 MI 1951	12x AMX-13 SS11		12e Régiment d'Artillerie
	153e Régiment d'Infanterie Mécanisée	56x AMX-13 VTT M56			16x 105mm AU
8e Brigade Mécanisée	8e Régiment de Dragons	54x AMX-13 MI 1951	12x AMX-13 SS11		61e Régiment d'Artillerie
	151e Régiment d'Infanterie Mécanisée	56x AMX-13 VTT M56			16x 105mm AU
total		108x M47, 108x AMX-13 MI 1951, 168x AMX-13 VTT M56	48x AMX-13 SS11		48x 105mm AU
8e Division Mécanisée (Réserve)* Compiègne					
2e Brigade Blindée	501e Régiment de Chars de Combat	54 x M47	12x AMX-13 SS11	12x AMX-13 VTT M56*	3e Régiment d'Artillerie de Marine
	503e Régiment de Chars de Combat	54 x M47	12x AMX-13 SS11	12x AMX-13 VTT M56*	16x 105mm AU
	Régiment de Marche du Tchad	56x AMX-13 VTT M56			
14e Brigade Mécanisée	16e Régiment de Dragons	54x AMX-13 MI 1951	12x AMX-13 SS11		41e Régiment d'Artillerie de Marine
	21e Régiment d'Infanterie de Marine	56x AMX-13 VTT M56			16x 105mm AU
10e Brigade Mécanisée	18e Régiment de Dragons	54x AMX-13 MI 1951	12x AMX-13 SS11		40e Régiment d'Artillerie
	1e Groupe de Chasseurs Mécanisé	56x AMX-13 VTT M56			16x 105mm AU
total		108x M47, 108x AMX-13 MI 1951, 168x AMX-13 VTT M56	48x AMX-13 SS11		48x 105mm AU

* 8e Division was reserve based in France, not on full war establishment, and last priority for some equipment

AFV totals Division 1959

540x M47,
378x AMX-13 MI 1951,
204x AMX-13 SS11,
792x AMX-13 M56 VTT,
192x 105mm AU

Material 3: Until the VTT M56 became available, the APC requirement was filled with US Haltracks

192x 105mm AU were required on paper, but it is possible that towed 105mm or M7 GMC were on strength in some units at the time that the Division 1959 was instituted

The *Division 1959* system proved hard to implement despite the improvements it represented. The cost of the war in Algeria made the expense of re-equipping the army in Europe unwelcome. Weapons like the AMX13 SS11 were received much later than anticipated in the *Régiment de Chars Légers* and the Mle 51's modernization or replacement was deferred. The 1962 Evian accords that marked the ending of the Algerian war effectively disbanded many units repatriated from Algeria and prevented the army from completing a smooth transition into the new divisional structure. North African regiments serving in Algeria were simply dissolved upon their return at Sissonnes in May 1963, or retitled as French cavalry and infantry regiments (which in turn had to be dissolved with chaotic consequences). Armoured units received priority for equipment wherever possible but the *Division 1959*s were only completed in the middle of the 1960s not long before the army was re-organised again in 1967. By that time the AMX30 was being introduced to replace the M47 and the Mle 51 in the *Arme Blindée Cavalerie*. To meet the challenges of the 1970s the AMX13 Mle 51 was modernised beginning a new career as the *fer de lance* of the mechanised infantry.[20]

This is a fine photo of an early production Mle 51 with the Type 2A chassis. These vehicles were in production from around 1954 and began to appear that year in completely re-equipped regiments. (*Thomas Seignon*)

By the late 1950s the final batches of Mle 51s delivered for French orders consisted of vehicles based on the Type 2D chassis. This fine overhead view shows the late features standardized on that chassis. Many such late model Mle 51s were reconfigured as AMX13 SS11 TCMs in the period 1963–1964. (*Thomas Seignon*)

An AMX13 crew of the *3e Régiment de Spahis Algériens* arrayed for inspection with regulation small arms. The first half of the 1960s was a golden age for the AMX13. Mle 51 deliveries were complete, tactics and unit structure seemed ideal, and several upgrades had been tried and tested. Funding issues, however, delayed all of the upgrades that could have been implemented and forced the army to streamline its divisional structures in the second half of the decade. (*Bernard Canonne*)

This photo was taken at a driving school course given at Bitche in 1966. The Mle 51 was a speedy and manoeuvrable vehicle but the crew would have been sorely bounced around during cross country operations. On flat ground the AMX13 was one of the faster tracked vehicles of its time. (*Bernard Canonne*)

AMX13 Mle 51 and VTT Mle 56s of *6e Régiment de Dragons* photographed during a pause during *Exercise Berthier*, conducted over open countryside in 1966 or 1967. The Mle 51 is a Type 2C Chassis with some upgraded features but still wearing the original idler wheel and lacking infrared equipment. (*Bernard Canonne*)

By 1966-67 most of the ABC's *Régiments de Chars Légers* that had operated under the Division 1959 system were preparing to convert to the AMX30B along with the Patton regiments, and those that continued as AMX13 units were preparing to stand a squadron of tanks down to be replaced by two squadrons of VTT Mle 56s. The notable exception was the 11e RCh in Berlin who kept 3 full squadrons of tanks; the introduction of the 3 tank platoon and the smaller 13 tank squadron was, however, universal. (*Bernard Canonne*)

This photo was taken in West Germany in the first half of the 1960s with the *3e Régiment de Spahis Algériens* or their successor regiment the *6e Régiment de Dragons; it* shows an Mle 51 built on the 2A chassis with some updated features such as the turret bellows type seals. (*Bernard Canonne*)

Chapter Nine

The AMX13 SS-11

The first major upgrade of the Mle 51's antitank capabilities in French service saw its transformation into a missile launching tank destroyer. This was achieved by mounting four wire-guided Nord Aviation SS11 missiles on rails above the main armament. DEFA had originally intended for the SS11 to be launched from the AMX13 VTT personnel carrier and from older tank types such as the M24 Chaffee (a concept tested successfully in November 1956). The proposed modification of the M24 into a missile tank included the replacement of its turret with a special turret mounting 6 SS11 missiles in ready position, a 90mm howitzer and a machine gun. A further 6 missiles were intended to be carried as reloads. A Mle 51 with twin 3-missile launchers was also tested in January 1957 but all other options were made to look unduly complex after an officer from the CTEB at Mailly designed a simple 4-missile launch rail system that could fit a standard FL10 turret with minimal modification. This simple expedient was tested on five modified Mle 51s in September 1957. DEFA next proposed a special SS11 launcher turret to be carried on the chassis of the turreted version of the Au 105mm self-propelled howitzer, armed with a 20mm cannon and launcher rails. By early 1958 the choice of how to best deploy the SS11 had been extended to launcher vehicles based on the tiny Hotchkiss APC. The system based on the AMX13 Mle 51 first proposed by the CTEB was finally adopted in April 1960; production, however, was slow and the first deliveries were only made in January 1963. By mid-1964 the *30e Régiment de Dragons* had completed troop trials and the AMX13 SS11 began to be issued.[21]

The SS11 had an average flight speed of 160 m/s and a range of 3,000 metres; with a penetration of 660 mm, it could destroy any tank in service at the time. Use of the weapon from the AMX13 platform presented some important limitations. The SS11 had to be fired in areas with a clear line of sight to the target and the flight path could not be obstructed by heavy scrub or trees. The missile aimer had to concentrate on flying the SS11 onto the target which usually made the weapon's best use from ambush positions. The first version of the AMX13 SS11 employed a manual command to line of sight (MCLOS) guidance system known as the TCM (for *Télécommande Manuelle*, using the T9C joystick control system). The commander controlled the SS11 in flight using a joystick. To house the T9C control, a stowage box was added on the left rear of the hull as space was not available elsewhere. The MAC31 machine gun was also replaced with the belt-fed AA52 machine gun to make space for the missile system's sighting equipment inside the turret. The SS11 TCM conversions were undertaken at the *4e Echelon* workshops at Gien on new Type 2D chassis vehicles and later on earlier production AMX13s fitted with the FL10D turret. The conversion included complete component disassembly and renovation for the hull and turret. All of the early hulls converted received the new production features seen on the 2C or 2D type hulls. These rebuilt vehicles could be distinguished by the new *immatriculation* with eight replacing four as the third digit.

In the middle of the 1960s the SS11's fire controls were improved by the provision of a semi-automatic command to line of sight guidance (or SACLOS known as the *Télécommande Automatique*, or TCA). The gunner now aimed his sight at the missile target and missile was slaved to its line of sight. The T10K joystick controller was used by commander exclusively to steer the missile if required. The TCA reduced the workload of the missile operator as he was no longer required to steer the missile but only to keep the cross-hairs of his sight on the target. With the modifications for the TCA fire control system the designation of the FL10 turret carried by the conversions was changed to FL10E. SS11 conversions included all four chassis types of Series 2 Mle 51s. In the cavalry AMX13 SS11 TCA and TCM conversions were deployed in equal numbers in a single squadron of twelve vehicles in each *régiment de chars légers*, and in each *régiment blindé* equipped with M47 Pattons. After the Division 1967 reorganization, a platoon of four AMX13 SS11s was assigned to each of the two squadrons of AMX13 C90s assigned to each *régiment d'infanterie mecanisée*. That same year a similar proposal to fire six HOT missiles from the FL10 turret of a modified AMX13 Mle 51 was tested and proven, but no orders ensued. The SS11 was not retained in the order of battle of the armoured regiments that were re-equipped with the AMX30 because of the improved antitank performance of the latter's CN-105-F1 gun.

This AMX13 SS11 was photographed in late 1963 at Le Valdahon where the returned 30e RD were based. Note the 2D type chassis and the missile lead wires. It was probably one of the first such conversions delivered to be used to conduct SS11 courses for several regiments. Only 2 SS11 missiles are fitted. A tarped-over Panhard EBR is parked in the background. (*Juan Gillard*)

This AMX13 SS11 was converted from a Type 2B or Type 2C chassis. From this angle we cannot see the tell-tale roof mounted SACLOS sight of an AMX13 SS11 TCA conversion so it is difficult to define the sub-type of this tank. (*Thomas Seignon*)

Removal of AMX13 SS11 No. 253's turret. This photo was taken by *aspirant* Guy Gibeau on the tank park of the *2e Escadron, 8e Groupe de Chasseurs Mécanisés* in 1973. (*Guy Gibeau*)

The 2/8GCM's SS11 platoon's tanks turrets being removed for routine maintenance. These are AMX13 SS11 TCA tank destroyers. (*Guy Gibeau*)

A Berliet heavy wrecker lifting AMX13 SS11 TCA No. 253's turret in 1973. (*Guy Gibeau*)

Vehicle batteries and hull ammunition racks are visible as maintenance took place after turrets were removed from their hulls. An inevitable task was to clean the accumulated dirt and grime that collected inside the fighting compartment under the turret basket. (*Guy Gibeau*)

An AMX13 SS11 TCM based on a Type 2D chassis. This tank, photographed in 1978, belonged to the SS11 platoon of the *4e Escadron*, 8e GCM. By 1978 the divisional structure had changed yet again, doing away with the brigade command level entirely. (*Guy Gibeau*)

This AMX13 SS11 TCM is seen without its missile armament manoeuvring at speed on a training area in 1978. Once its missiles were fired the AMX13 SS11 had the same firepower as an unmodified AMX13 Mle 51. After the 1977 divisional reorganization the regimental titles of the mechanized infantry regiments changed. The 8e GCM was thereafter designated simply the *8e Groupe de Chasseurs*. (*Guy Gibeau*)

The SS11 platoon of the 2/8GC seen in September 1979. Unlike the 3-tank AMX13 C90 platoons, the 4-tank SS11 platoon operated as two fire teams with two missile launching tanks each. (*Guy Gibeau*)

Full NBC protective gear was worn by these AMX13 SS11 crewmen in a 1979 exercise. Note how the SS11 missiles are dismounted and their launch rails are covered. One of the wire mesh protection guards for the missiles has been removed from the nearest vehicle and we can see the attachment points. The Mle 51 was far too small to carry an NBC system and predated such design requirements. (*Guy Gibeau*)

The exterior mounting ramp fittings for the SS11 were common to all of the AMX13 SS11 conversions. (*Guy Gibeau*)

The Nord Aviation SS11 missile was first tested in 1954 and was mass produced until 1984. The SS11 was assembled from the missile body and warhead in the field and also existed in a version that could be fired from helicopters. (*Guy Gibeau*)

The AMX13 SS11 was the first ATGM missile launching tank introduced in numbers in any NATO army. Its use was dependent on carefully handled logistics and resupply points. (*Guy Gibeau*)

An AMX13 SS11 TCA of the 2/8GC at the moment of firing in 1980. Fitting the SS11 as a weapon fired from the AMX13 Mle 51's FL10 turret required internal modifications such as the installation of electronics, and the re-equipping the missile's sighting and fire control system. (*Guy Gibeau*)

FL10 turrets modified to fire the SS11 with the TCM system kept their FL10 Type D designation; those modified for the more elaborate TCA fire control system were designated FL10 Type E. This spectacular shot shows 2 AMX13 SS11 TCAs firing on the Suippes ranges at night in 1980. (*Guy Gibeau*)

Most conversions were made on vehicles that were scheduled for rebuilding, and included Mle 51s built on the Series 2A, 2B and 2C chassis. A mixed group of AMX13 SS11s from the 2/8GC are seen here in January 1980 at the Mailly ranges. (*Guy Gibeau*)

An AMX13 SS11 TCA of the *Peloton Gibeau*, *2e Escadron*, 8e GC in October 1980 at the Suippes firing range loading a missile onto one of the launcher rails. (*Guy Gibeau*)

This SS11 platoon, like all AMX13 SS11 platoons, was made up of 2 fire teams each comprising a pair of missile launch vehicles. In the mechanized infantry one SS11 platoon was integral to each of the 2 tank squadrons. (*Guy Gibeau*)

A crewman from the 2/8GC carrying a practice missile at the Suippes ranges in 1980. (*Guy Gibeau*)

An AMX13 SS11 TCA converted from an Mle 51 originally delivered on the 2A chassis. It was serving with the 3e escadron of the *30e Groupe de Chasseurs* when photographed here in 1979. It carries no missiles and is parked on a firing range. The new NATO marking adopted in early 1979 is visible on the left front mudguard. (*Thierry Laroche*)

The 30 GC was reformed at Luneville in 1968 and served as a motorized infantry regiment until the Division 1977 system was implemented. It duly received tracked APCs, and 2 squadrons of AMX13 C90s and AMX13 SS11s. The 30 GC served as one of the 2 mechanized infantry regiments in the *4e Division Blindée* at that time. (*Thierry Laroche*)

An AMX13 SS11 of the *30e Groupe de Chasseurs* in 1979. The crewman on the turret is wearing the dark blue shirt worn in Chasseur regiments (mechanized or alpine) prior to the introduction of the *chemise modèle F1* and carries an MAT49 submachine gun. (*Thierry Laroche*)

The success of the AMX13 SS11 TCA, a very advanced weapon for the mid-1960s, resulted from its simplicity. Later missile tanks were weapons normally bedevilled by complexity; significant problems were encountered when the French attempted to mount the ACRA missile in the AMX30. In the United States major issues arose with the Shillelagh missile system employed in the M551 and M60A2. (*Thierry Laroche*)

The last AMX13 SS11s left French service at the end of the Cold War. (*Thierry Laroche*)

The 43e RIMa (*Régiment d'Infanterie de Marine* – Marine Infantry Regiment) was garrisoned at the Offenburg barracks in Germany until its disbandment in 1977/78. It participated actively in the tasks entrusted to the *FFA* (French Forces in Germany) and did numerous rotations in Berlin. The regiment had 2 infantry companies with 3 sections of 4 VTTs, 2 squadrons of AMX13 C90s (4 platoons of 3 tanks each) and a single platoon of 4 AMX13 SS11s. (*Peter Lau Collection*)

Chapter Ten

The AMX13 C90

At the same time as the 105mm gun was being fitted into the FL-10 to create the Mle 58 the cheaper option of modifying the CN-75-50 to fire 90mm ammunition was also examined. The French army had this option available from 1962 onwards but, due to a number of factors (including the perfection of the 90mm hollow charge round's ballistics at high velocity), the existing Mle 51 fleet was only upgraded in 1964. Funding shortfalls further delayed conversions until June 1966. The 90mm option followed an interesting development path marked by thrift and resourcefulness.[22]

In the late 1950s French Army required a light infantry support vehicle (the *Engin Léger de Combat*) armed with a 90mm gun which was expected to also arm the new Panhard AML 90 light armoured car. The round developed for these light vehicles was originally a powerful Obus-G, but due to the cost of new guns and the cost of manufacturing these relatively complex rounds for two types of gun, it was decided to proceed with a simple fin stabilized hollow charge round instead. This was known as the OCC-90-62 (*obus à charge creuse empenné de 90 mm modèle 1962*). The ELC was cancelled but its gun was chosen to arm the Panhard AML-90 armoured car. Re-boring the CN-75-SA-49 to fire ammunition fired by the new 90mm gun was later proposed successfully as an upgrade for the EBR's FL11 turret and the process was applied to modernize the Mle 51.[23]

The *Atelier de Bourges* re-bored the CN-75-50 gun to fire the new 90mm hollow charge ammunition. The re-bored gun was designated D960 and was standardized as the CN-90-F3. As it was a longer barrelled weapon than the EBR90's re-bored D924 gun it could fire the aluminum shelled 90mm round further and with greater accuracy at a muzzle velocity of 950 meters per second. The CN-90-F3 gun's antitank performance approached that of the CN-105-57 carried by the AMX13 Mle 58 and the gun could be provided to the existing Mle 51 fleet at a fraction of the cost. The 90mm OCC-90-62 round weighed approximately half as much as an Obus G of similar calibre and the gun had much lower chamber pressure and recoil. The light OCC-90-62 projectile and the long barrel of the CN-90-F3 actually gave it a slightly longer range than the Mle 58's gun. The *Atelier de Puteaux* tested a ranging gun to enable accurate long range fire with the CN-90-F3 but results were no better than for the Mle 58. The CN-90-F3 did not require a muzzle brake due to the reduced chamber pressure but it kept the original muzzle brake which channelled muzzle blast and smoke from the gunner's sight.[24]

The CN-90-F3 was fitted with a thermal sleeve and the modified tanks were designated *AMX 13 tonnes 90 F1* or *Char 13 t – 90 – F1*, but the unofficial designation AMX13 C90 was also generally adopted. In all 875 Mle 51s (15 of which were sold to Tunisia) were converted from 1966 and into the 1970s at the EFAB Bourges. In 1966 it was expected that 3 regiments worth of AMX13 C90 conversions could be undertaken each year. The AMX13 C90 effectively replaced nearly all of the 75mm Mle 51 light tanks (excepting the SS11 conversions) in French army service during the 1970s; a fine example of a successful modernization program that extended the little tank's career in France by twenty years.

The other upgrades standardized with the 90mm gun conversion included an infra-red projector mounted on the turret roof, a DI-VT-2A infra-red sight for the gunner, and infra-red driving lights. The FL10 turret's original telescopic sights were retained for want of better fire controls. The AMX13 C90's introduction coincided with the implementation of the Division 1967 system and the upgraded vehicle became standard equipment for two squadrons in each of the *régiments d'infanterie mecanisée* and *groupes de chasseurs mécanisées*. The remaining 75mm-armed tanks and all AMX13 SS11 conversions were brought up to the standard of the AMX13 C90 (with infrared night vision equipment) in 1967. The AMX13 C90 conversion allowed the AMX13 to remain in service as a gun tank well into the 1980s.[25]

The *1e Peloton* (1st Platoon) of the 2/8GCM was equipped with AMX13 C90s. These turrets have been removed for maintenance, a necessity caused by the diminutive size of the AMX13's hull. (*Guy Gibeau*)

Another 1973 photo showing the suspended turret of one of the 8e GCM's AMX13 C90s. The turret was hoisted up with a dedicated lifting bar attached to lifting rings on the turret face and bustle. (*Guy Gibeau*)

Crewmen of the *1e Peloton, 2e Escadron, 8e Groupe de Chasseurs Mécanisés* in cold weather gear during *Maneuvre Honheim* 1973. This AMX13 C90 was converted from an AMX13 Series 2A2R, and it still carries many original features visible in the slanted tool boxes and running gear. (*Guy Gibeau*)

Another view of the same tank (288 0415) showing the mix of features so typical for C90 conversions. The CN-90-F3 was an effective tank killer and the conversion was well regarded by its crews. (*Guy Gibeau*)

An AMX13 C90 of the 2/8GCM embarked for rail transport during a move to a training area in 1973. The AMX13 was easily secured for rail travel and, for long distance unit movements, this kept mechanical wear to a minimum. (*Guy Gibeau*)

Track maintenance on an AMX13 C90 of the 8e GCM at Mailly in June 1973. (*Guy Gibeau*)

Mounted on a rail car at Mailly in the summer of 1973, this AMX13 C90's rear left side and track guard details are visible. The vehicle was delivered as a Type 2A chassis and converted after 1966. Some detail is visible for the attachment of the rear turret joint bellows cover, the rear of the smoke discharger mounts and the reflector mounted on the rear track guards. (*Guy Gibeau*)

Front view of a different tank built originally on a Type 2B or 2C chassis. The AMX13 was chocked and secured to the railway flatcar by chains and turnbuckles lashed to eyes on the railcar chassis. (*Guy Gibeau*)

The helmeted gunner and driver of the *adjoint*'s tank, 1e Peleton, 2/8GCM in 1974. The *adjoint* was the second in command of the tank platoon, equivalent in function to a troop sergeant in a British or Commonwealth army tank troop. This AMX13 C90 was converted from an Mle 51 with the Type 2A chassis. It carries the regimental crest of the *8e Groupe de Chasseurs Mécanisés* on the left front fender, cover over the muzzle and map tucked over the commander's sight. (*Guy Gibeau*)

This view of an AMX13 C90 based on a Type 2B chassis of the same platoon in early 1974 shows the full range of markings carried by an AMX13 serving in a mechanized infantry regiment in a type 1967 armoured division. On the front right of the turret is the yellow bridge classification disc; next to it the white disc with the number 3 showing is the railway loading classification. The front hull is marked with the *numéro d'immatriculation* and the front left trackguard carries the 8e GCM's yellow and green hunting horn regimental device. (*Guy Gibeau*)

A colour photo of the 2/8GCM on the ranges at Mussingen in June 1974. This is the *1e Peleton* firing with AMX13 C90s. The empty 90mm case has been thrown out of the turret ejection port of call sign 203 (based on a 2B chassis) and we can see the red warning flag on the turret roof. The regimental insignia is carried on the turret rear, along with the tactical number. The tarpaulin rack is on the rear hull plate. (*Guy Gibeau*)

Call sign 211 firing, with the commander sitting braced low down in his cupola directing the gunner with binoculars. This AMX13 C90 is based on a Type 2A chassis, and the track appears slack, possibly because the recoil has rocked the tank backwards. (*Guy Gibeau*)

Tank crews of the 2/8GCM cleaning their 90mm guns after a range exercise. (*Guy Gibeau*)

The muzzle brake used on the CN-75-50 was recycled as a blast and smoke deflector when the Mle 51s were refitted with the lower pressure CN-90-F3 gun – simply a modified and re-bored CN-75-50. This is the muzzle brake of tank 288 0415. (*Guy Gibeau*)

While the gunnery centre at Trier in West Germany was an important location for training AMX13 gunners, a second location staffed by the *Arme Blindée Cavalerie* at Canjuers assumed greater importance in the late 1970s and remains in use today. This photo was taken in May 1978 and it shows 8e GC crews preparing to load ammunition into an AMX13's automatic loading system. (*Guy Gibeau*)

The two *barillets* that fed the AMX13's guns could be reloaded through the turret roof loading doors on each side of the turret bustle roof. Rounds would be handed up to a crewman standing on the vehicle and loaded in one by one. (*Guy Gibeau*)

If manpower permitted, the two *barillets* could be loaded at the same time. (*Guy Gibeau*)

The vehicle commander ensures that the rounds are loaded properly just prior to the firing period. In a conscript army this type of task was supervised by experienced regulars and safety precautions were taken very seriously. (*Guy Gibeau*)

Boresighting the gun was another essential step that was always conducted prior to a firing period. (*Guy Gibeau*)

The *Pas de Tir des Amandiers* at Canjuers. Located in southern France, Canjuers offered excellent gunnery ranges and a manoeuvre area unencumbered by civilians. Crews of the 8e GC receive their pre range period briefings in May 1978. (*Guy Gibeau*)

After the briefing the platoon is ready to mount up and advance to the *pas de tir*. (*Guy Gibeau*)

Fire! The blast of the CN-90-F3 firing was followed by the ejection of a hot brass casing. The fin stabilized *Obus Charge Creuse* OCC-90-62 was the standard antitank projectile for the AML90, the EBR90 and the AMX13-90-F1 (known as often as not as the AMX13 C90 to its crews). Guns in each vehicle varied and consequently their performance firing the hollow charge rounds was also different. (*Guy Gibeau*)

The *Centre de Perfectionnement du Tir* at Trier also kept a few turretless Mle 51s as improvised driver trainers much as disarmed AMX-US tanks were employed on some French training bases. The turretless driver trainer was commonly known as the 'AMX Ben Hur' after the charioteer of Hollywood movie fame. This one has the Type 2C chassis. (*Guy Gibeau*)

This pair of 'AMX Ben Hurs' photographed in 1978 were based on older Type 2A chassis that had originally been converted into AMX13 C90s. It is unknown if the turrets were eventually refitted or if they were permanent conversions. (*Guy Gibeau*)

An AMX13 C90 of the 8eGC seen at Trier in 1978. In 1978-1980 most of the remaining AMX13-equipped regiments in the *Arme Blindée Cavalerie* re-equipped with the AMX30B. This left the vast majority of AMX13 C90s and AMX13 SS11s in the French army in the mechanized infantry which itself was in course of adopting the new AMX10P. (*Guy Gibeau*)

Left: This overhead shot was taken at the *Stade de Tir* 7 at the CPT at Trier, West Germany, in 1978. The thermal jacket fitted to the CN-90-F3 ensured that the barrel's temperature remained constant during protracted fire. This vehicle is based on a Type 2A or 2A2R chassis. We can see the gun mantlet casting clearly marked with the SFAC casting mark, typical for most Mle 51s. The top of the turret, or *corps oscillant*, was formed from a fabricated rear section welded to a frontal casting. (*Guy Gibeau*)

Below: By 1984, when this photo was taken' the AMX13 C90 was being replaced in the mechanized infantry units in the FFA (*Forces Francaises en Allemagne*, or French Forces in Germany) and nearing the end of its career in mechanized regiments in France. This vehicle belongs to the *2e Escadron, 150e Régiment d'Infanterie*. (*Guy Gibeau*)

Although the stock of parts supporting the AMX13 fleet was still reasonably large multiple rebuilds made some vehicles beyond economic repair. (*Guy Gibeau*)

The *Division 1984* instituted that year marked the change to a single tank squadron in the mechanized infantry regiments. The AMX13 C90 was by then a logistic anomaly in units equipped with the diesel powered AMX10P and was long overdue for retirement. Its numbers dwindled in the next year as it was replaced by the AMX30B. (*Guy Gibeau*)

River crossing was a specialty practised with enthusiasm in the FFA. This 1981 photo shows elements of the 8e GC's 2e Escadron embarked for crossing on a pontoon ferry. Here, 3 AMX13 C90s, a VTT Mle 56 and a Hotchkiss Jeep. (*Guy Gibeau*)

The 30e GC, like the other mechanized infantry regiments in the *Divisions 1967* and *Divisions 1977*, included 2 squadrons of AMX13 C90s and 2 companies of APC borne infantry. The AMX13 C90 in the foreground was based on a 2B or 2C chassis and belonged to the *1e Escadron*, photographed here in June 1978 at Mailly. (*Jean Ancher*)

Loading the 90mm rounds employed with the CN-90-F1 was much the same as loading the older 75mm ammunition. The shell casing was adapted to the OCC Mle 62 round without significant difficulties and the ammunition did not require any modification of the automatic loading system because the casing size and overall dimensions remained the same as those used for the 75mm rounds. (Jean Ancher)

An AMX13 C90 of the 1/30 GC on the firing ranges at Mailly in 1978. The empty shell casing is thrown clear from the automatic loader ejection port in the turret rear. This vehicle is based on an Mle 51 built on the Series 2A chassis. (Jean Ancher)

After 1984 the 30e GC adopted the Division 1984 order of battle, which theoretically required 1 squadron of 17 tanks and 3 companies of mechanized infantry in AMX10Ps. This made a substantial number of AMX13 C90s redundant and most of the VTT Mle 56 fleet was retired (excepting command post and ambulance vehicles). In the 30e GC the remaining tanks served in the 3e Escadron. Here an AMX13 C90 is training in the outskirts of Luneville in September 1986. (*Jean Ancher*)

Cross country manoeuvres with the 3/30e GC in September 1986. This vehicle was over 30 years old and one of only about 60 AMX13 C90s left in the mechanized infantry regiments. The AMX13 SS11s were removed from the mechanized regiments and were used to form divisional antitank companies. Between 1984 and 1987 all AMX13 C90s left in Europe were serving in mechanized infantry units based in France until these were also replaced by AMX30Bs. (*Jean Ancher*)

Chapter Eleven

The Division 1967

From 1967 until the end of its career in the French Army, the AMX13 served predominantly in the mechanized infantry. As noted with regard to the 90mm and the SS11 conversions over 1,200 vehicles upgraded from the Mle 51 were retained in service into the 1970s. More fundamental than the appearance of new tanks or the retention of the AMX13 to the cavalry regiments was the comprehensive change in squadron structure that came with the Division 1967 reorganization. Since 1943 French armoured squadrons had been built on the basis of the 5-tank platoon which had enjoyed a freedom of action that changed with the introduction of the 3-tank platoon and its emphasis on tighter squadron-level control. This change in doctrine accompanied the 1967 army reorganization and the tactics adopted in the *Régiment de Chars 54* (RC54) and in the mechanized regiment tank squadrons reflected tighter control at regimental level.

Divisions 1967 were also organized with three mechanized brigades; each theoretically included an RC54 armoured regiment (with four squadrons of AMX-30s) and two mechanized regiments with two squadrons of thirteen AMX13 C90s and two companies of infantry mounted in VTT Mle 56 armoured personnel carriers. The tactical wartime doctrine in the mechanized infantry was for each tank squadron to exchange a platoon of three tanks for a section of VTT borne infantry from a mechanized infantry company (a system that worked well on the tactical level). Each division had a nuclear artillery regiment armed with four SRBM launchers and the AMX13 crews were expected to rely on gas masks and NBC suits for their personal protection on a contaminated battlefield. No fewer than 3,000 AMX13 series vehicles were required for the five *Divisions 1967*.[26]

Despite the introduction of the more capable AMX30 into service from early 1967, production of the new tank was slow. The AMX13 group shrunk very quickly once the French Army's orders for Mle 51s and VTT Mle 56 orders were completed. FCM, which was suffering from the decline in naval orders and the inability to modernize its facilities, dropped out in 1965 and closed down in 1966. AMX and the *Atelier de Roanne* became focused on the AMX30 and a new generation of lighter AFVs. Foreign AMX13 orders were produced at SFAC, which became Creusot Loire Industries in 1970. The few cavalry regiments that retained the AMX13 C90 after the AMX30 was introduced formed part of the general reserve in France, or part of the training establishment, excepting the *11e Régiment de Chasseurs* stationed in West Berlin. These units retained the AMX13 into the late 1970s (and in some cases the 1980s) even after the *Division 1977* was adopted.

Escadron de Chars de 13 Tonnes, AMX13 C90, Régiment Mécanisé, Division 1967

Peloton de Commandement Headquarters Platoon

100 VTT PC 101 105 VTT for *groupe échelon* (light aid detachment)

1e Peloton tank platoon

111 112 113

2e Peloton tank platoon

121 122 123 **Total: 13x 90mm CN-90-F3, 4x CN-75-50, 16x SS11**

3e Peloton tank platoon

131 132 133

4e Peloton tank platoon

141 142 143

Peloton SS11 TCM (for first tank squadron)   *Peloton SS11 TCA* (for second tank squadron)

151 152 *1e groupe de tir*   151 152 *1e groupe de tir*

153 154 *2e groupe de tir*   153 154 *2e groupe de tir*

155 *groupe munitions* missile reloads   155 *groupe munitions* missile reloads

The *1e Régiment de Chasseurs* was based at Montbéliard from 1964 to 1969, equipped with Mle 51s. From 1969 until 31 July 1976, the regiment was relocated to Phalsbourg and reorganized along the same lines as a *régiment mécanisé* and was issued AMX13 C90s. The *4e Régiment de Dragons* received the AMX13 C90 in April 1968 and was equipped along the same pattern as a *regiment mecanisé* until June 1979 at Olivet, south of Orleans. When the 4e RD was dissolved on 30 June 1979, the *18e Régiment de Dragons*, equipped since 1973 with AMX30Bs at Mourmelon, assumed their regimental title. The *5e Régiment de Dragons* were equipped with AMX13 Mle 51s from June 1964 until July 1968 at Friedrichshaven. They re-equipped with AMX13 C90s along the same pattern as a *regiment mecanisée* and moved to Tübingen on 31 August 1968. The AMX13 C90s were retained until the regiment was

An AMX13 C90 with Type C chassis as seen in May 1984 during a parade at Quartier Lepic of the E.A.I. (L'Ecole d'Apllication de l'Infanterie) at Montpellier. (*Peter Lau Collection*)

dissolved on 31 August 1978. The 30th *Régiment de Dragons* at Valdahon (already equipped with AMX30Bs) assumed their regimental title on 1 September 1978. The *11e Régiment de Chasseurs* were equipped with the Mle 51 from 1955 and converted to the AMX13 C90 in the early 1970s. Stationed in Berlin, the 11e RCh kept the AMX13 in service through the army reorganizations of 1967. The unit was unique after 1967 in keeping the AMX13 Mle 51 (and subsequently the AMX13 C90) in all 3 squadrons and this continued until 1983.

The AMX13's role in the *Division 1967* represented the high tide of the AMX13's use in the French army despite its progressive disappearance from the cavalry as a first line weapon. The *Division 1977* marked the beginning of a steady decline in the number of AMX13 based vehicles in French service. New AFV types like the tracked AMX10P, the Au F1 artillery system and the wheeled VAB were introduced as partial or complete replacements for APC and artillery variants in the 1970s and in the early 1980s. These did not much affect the role of the AMX13 C90 but steadily replaced the VTT Mle 56, the OB-105-AU Mle 50 and the AM F3. The Division 1977 also did away with the entire brigade based formation to cut costs and created eight smaller divisions to replace five larger ones.

Cavalry and mechanized infantry units still equipped with the AMX 13 kept their 1967 regimental structure until 1984. At the beginning of 1982 the first AMX30Bs were issued to the

Division 1967 and Brigades

1e Division Mécanisée

	Artillery, Mechanised Infantry and Armoured Regiments	AMX30B	AMX13 C90	AMX13 SS11	AMX13 VTT Mle 56*	AMX13 SANITAIRE	AMX13 Mle 55	OB 105 Mle 50 AU	155 Am F3	AMX-13 RATAC	AMX Bitube 30mm	VCG	PP Mle 57
(Divisional assets)	13e Régiment du Génie				12	?	?					12	4
	51e Régiment d'Artillerie				5	?	?				9		
	68° Régiment d'Artillerie Lourde Divisionnaire				18	1	1	15					
1e Brigade Mécanisée	1e Régiment de Cuirassiers	54			19	2							
	16e Groupe de Chasseurs Mécanisé		26	8	36	2	2						
	2e Groupe de Chasseurs Mécanisé		26	8	36	2	2						
	9e Régiment d'Artillerie de Marine				18	1	1		15	6			
3e Brigade Mécanisée	5e Régiment de Cuirassiers	54			19	2							
	8e Groupe de Chasseurs Mécanisé		26	8	36	2	2						
	42e Régiment d'Infanterie Mécanisée		26	8	36	2	2						
	16e Régiment d'Artillerie				18	1	1		15	6			
11e Brigade Motorisée	6e Régiment de Dragons	54			19	2							
	7e Régiment d'Infanterie Motorisée	Information not available at time of writing											
	8e Régiment d'Infanterie Motorisée	Information not available at time of writing											
	2e Régiment d'Artillerie				18	1	1	15					
division orbat AMX		**162**	**104**	**32**	**290**	**18**	**12**	**30**	**30**	**12**	**9**	**12**	**4**

3e Division Mécanisée

	Artillery, Mechanised Infantry and Armoured Regiments	AMX30B	AMX13 C90	AMX13 SS11	AMX13 VTT Mle 56*	AMX13 SANITAIRE	AMX13 Mle 55	OB 105 Mle 50 AU	155 Am F3	AMX-13 RATAC	AMX Bitube 30mm	VCG	PP Mle 57
(Divisional assets)	32e Régiment du Génie				12	?	?					12	4
	53e Régiment d'Artillerie				5	?	?				9		
	32° Régiment d'Artillerie Lourde Divisionnaire				18	1	1	15					
5e Brigade Mécanisée	2e Régiment de Cuirassiers	54			19	2							
	5e Régiment de Dragons		26	8	36	2	2						
	24e Groupe de Chasseurs Mécanisé		26	8	36	2	2						
	73e Régiment d'Artillerie				18	1	1		15	6			
12e Brigade Mécanisée	12e Régiment de Cuirassiers	54			19	2							
	43e Régiment Blindé d'Infanterie de Marine		26	8	36	2	2						
	19e Groupe de Chasseurs Mécanisé		26	8	36	2	2						
	11e Régiment d'Artillerie				18	1	1		15	6			
13e Brigade Motorisée	5e Régiment de Hussards (EBR)												
	3e Régiment d'Infanterie Motorisée	Information not available at time of writing											
	129e Régiment d'Infanterie Motorisée	Information not available at time of writing											
	34e Régiment d'Artillerie				18	1	1	15					
division orbat AMX		**108**	**104**	**32**	**271**	**16**	**12**	**30**	**30**	**12**	**9**	**12**	**4**

4e Division Mécanisée

	Artillery, Mechanised Infantry and Armoured Regiments	AMX30B	AMX13 C90	AMX13 SS11	AMX13 VTT Mle 56*	AMX13 SANITAIRE	AMX13 Mle 55	OB 105 Mle 50 AU	155 Am F3	AMX-13 RATAC	AMX Bitube 30mm	VCG	PP Mle 57
(Divisional assets)	3e Régiment du Génie				12	?	?					12	4
	54e Régiment d'Artillerie				5	?	?				9		
	15° Régiment d'Artillerie Lourde Divisionnaire				18	1	1	15					
10e Brigade Mécanisée	503e Régiment de Chars de Combat	54			19	2	2						
	18e Régiment de Dragons		26	8	36	2	2						
	1e Groupe de Chasseurs Mécanisé		26	8	36	2	2						
	40e Régiment d'Artillerie				18	1	1		15	6			

Brigade	Regiment	C1	C2	C3	C4	C5	C6	C7	C8	C9	C10	C11	C12
15e Brigade Mécanisée	2e Régiment de Chasseurs	54			19				2	1			
	150e Régiment d'Infanterie Motorisée	Information not available at time of writing											
	94e Régiment d'Infanterie Motorisée	Information not available at time of writing											
	25e Régiment d'Artillerie	54			18	1	1	15	6				
16e Brigade Mécanisée	4e Régiment de Cuirassiers	54			19	2	2						
	8e Régiment de Dragons		26	8	36	2	2						
	151e Régiment d'Infanterie Mécanisée		26	8	36	2	2						
	61e Régiment d'Artillerie				18	1	1	15	15				
division orbat AMX		162	104	32	290	18	12	30	30	12	9	12	4

7e Division Mécanisée

Brigade	Regiment	C1	C2	C3	C4	C5	C6	C7	C8	C9	C10	C11	C12
(Divisional assets)	9e Régiment du Génie				12	?	?					12	4
	57e Régiment d'Artillerie				5						9		
	1° Régiment d'Artillerie Lourde Divisionnaire	Remark: towed 155mm											
6e Brigade Mécanisée	2e Régiment de Dragons	54			19	2	2						
	1e Régiment de Chasseurs		26	8	36	2	2						
	153e Régiment d'Infanterie Mécanisée		26	8	36	2	2						
	12e Régiment d'Artillerie				18	1	1	15					
7e Brigade Mécanisée	30e Régiment de Dragons	54			19	2	2						
	1e Régiment de Dragons		26	8	36	2	2						
	35e Régiment d'Infanterie Mécanisée		26	8	36	2	2						
	74e Régiment d'Artillerie				18	1	1	15					
8e Brigade Motorisée	3e Régiment de Cuirassiers	54			19	2							
	170e Régiment d'Infanterie Motorisée	Information not available at time of writing											
	30e Groupe de Chasseurs	Information not available at time of writing											
	8e Régiment d'Artillerie				18	1	1	15	45				
division orbat AMX		162	104	32	272	17	11	45	0	0	9	12	4

8e Division Mécanisée

Brigade	Regiment	C1	C2	C3	C4	C5	C6	C7	C8	C9	C10	C11	C12
(Divisional assets)	71e Régiment du Génie				12	?	?					12	4
	58e Régiment d'Artillerie				5						9		
2e Brigade Mécanisée	501e Régiment de Chars de Combat	54			19	2	2						
	4e Régiment de Dragons		26	8	36	2	2						
	Régiment de Marche du Tchad		26	8	36	2	2						
	1e Régiment d'Artillerie de Marine				18			15	6				
	7e Régiment de Chasseurs (AML)												
4e Brigade Motorisée	51e Régiment d'Infanterie Motorisée	Information not available at time of writing											
	67e Régiment d'Infanterie Motorisée	Information not available at time of writing											
	3e Régiment d'Artillerie de Marine	54			18	1	1	15					
14e Brigade Mécanisée	6e Régiment de Cuirassiers				19	2	2						
	16e Régiment de Dragons		26	8	36	2	2						
	21e Régiment d'Infanterie de Marine		26	8	36	2	2						
	41e Régiment d'Artillerie de Marine				18	1	1	15	6				
division orbat AMX		108	104	32	253	14	10	15	30	12	9	12	4

Total per AMX type	702	520	160	1376	83	57	150	120	48	45	60	20

Total (AMX13 series): 2639

(Remark: The actual figure is higher than this number as there are still 10 regiments worth of vehicles which are not accounted for due to lack of information.)

* VTT totals include APCs, Command Vehicles in armoured units and ammunition carriers in artillery units, and all other variants

Totals: 3000 AMX-13 series vehicles required for the 5 divisions, at minimum, including 1080 Light Tanks and SS11 Missile Launchers.

Division 1977

Régiment	AMX30B	AMX13 C90	AMX13 S11	AMX 10 P	VTT Mle 56 S470 ou CAFI38	VTT Mle 56 T20/13	VTT Mle 56 T20/13 MILAN	AMX-13 SANITAIRE	AMX-13 M55	VCG	155 Am F3	AMX-13 RATAC
1e Division Blindée												
1e Régiment de Cuirassiers	54			18								
6e Régiment de Dragons	54			18								
16e Groupe de Chasseurs		26	8		12	24	8	2	2			
8e Groupe de Chasseurs		26	8		12	24	8	2	2			
9e Régiment d'Artillerie de Marine					18			2	2		15	6
13e Régiment du Génie					12			?	?	12		
2e Division Blindée												
501e Régiment de Chars de Combat	54			18								
6e Régiment de Cuirassiers	54			18				2	2			
5e Régiment d'Infanterie		26	8		12	24	8	2	2			
Régiment de Marche du Tchad		26	8		12	24	8	2	2			
1e Régiment d'Artillerie Marine					18			2	2		15	6
34e Régiment du Génie					12			?	?	12		
3e Division Blindée												
3e Régiment de Dragons	54			18								
12e Régiment de Cuirassiers	54			18				2	2			
19e Groupe de Chasseurs		26	8		12	24	8	2	2			
42e Régiment d'Infanterie		26	8		12	24	8	2	2			
34e Régiment d'Artillerie					18			2	2		15	6
32e Régiment du Génie					12			?	?	12		
4e Division Blindée												
2e Régiment de Chasseurs	54			18								
3e Régiment de Cuirassiers	54			18				2	2			
30e Groupe de Chasseurs		26	8		12	24	8	2	2			
151e Régiment d'Infanterie		26	8		12	24	8	2	2			
61e Régiment d'Artillerie					18			2	2		15	6
6e Régiment du Génie					12			?	?	12		
5e Division Blindée												
2e Régiment de Cuirassiers	54			18				2	2			
5e Régiment de Cuirassiers	54			18				2	2			
2e Groupe de Chasseurs		26	8		12	24	8	2	2			
24e Groupe de Chasseurs		26	8		12	24	8	2	2			
24e Régiment d'Artillerie					18			2	2		15	6
11e Régiment du Génie					12			?	?	12		
6e Division Blindée												
2e Régiment de Dragons	54			18								
4e Régiment de Cuirassiers	54			18				2	2			
152e Régiment d'Infanterie		26	8		12	24	8	2	2			
153e Régiment d'Infanterie		26	8		12	24	8	2	2			
12e Régiment d'Artillerie					18			2	2		15	6
9e Régiment du Génie					12			?	?	12		

7e Division Blindée	1e Régiment de Dragons	54		18				2			
	30e Régiment de Dragons (2)	54		18				2			
	35e Régiment d'Infanterie	26	8		12	24	8	2	2		
	170e Régiment d'Infanterie	26	8		12	24	8	2	2		
	1e Régiment d'Artillerie				18			2		15	6
	19e Régiment du Génie				12			?	12		
10e Division Blindée	18e Régiment de Dragons (1)	54		18				2			
	503e Régiment de Chars de Combat	54		18				2			
	1e Groupe de Chasseurs (3)	26	8		8		8	2	2		
	150e Régiment d'Infanterie (3)	26	8	28	8		8	2	2		
	3e Régiment d'Artillerie de Marine				18			2		15	6
	3e Régiment du Génie				12			?	12		
Berlin	11e Régiment de Chasseurs (5)	41			8			2	2		
Olivet	4e Régiment de Dragons (4)										
NOTE	Artillery Regiments equipped with the 155 Am F3 received 4 batteries of guns from 1981				24			2	2	20	8

General:

The transformation from Division 1967 to Division 1977 took place over the January 1977 to July 1979 period. During this time, some regiments retained their 1967 structure and garrisons longer than others. Other regiments were renamed or dissolved.

Examples

(4) The 16e Régiment d'Artillerie did not leave Trier (FRG) for Melun (France) until July 1979.B64

The 4° Régiment de Dragons (Olivet), equipped with AMX13 C90s was dissolved in July 1979, and was replaced by the 6° Régiment de Cuirassiers, equipped with the AMX30B

The 6° Régiment de Cuirassiers based at Laon-Couvron (2°DB) was transferred to Olivet in July 1979.B66

(1) The 18° Régiment de Dragons at Mourmelon (10°DB) was renamed 4° Régiment de Dragons on August 1st 1979.

(2) The 30° Régiment de Dragons based at Valdahon (7°DB), was renamed as the 5° Régiment de Dragons on the 1st of August 1978.B68

The 3° Régiment d'Artillerie de Marine based at Vernon (10°DB) did not transfer to its new base at Verdun until July 1984

-The 42° Régiment d'Infanterie de Marine based at Offenburg (FRG) was dissolved in July 1978 and was replaced by the 42° Régiment d'Infanterie which moved from Wittlich (FRG) in August 1978

Exceptions

(3) In the Division 1977 structure, the 1°Groupe de Chasseurs and 150° Régiment d'Infanterie never received the VTT Mle 56 T20/13. The 1° Groupe de Chasseurs tested out the AMX10P in all four companies and in 1977, transferred 2 companies to the 150° Régiment d'Infanterie. Both regiments received 2 squadrons of AMX13 C90s from the 18° Régiment de Dragons.

(5) The 11° Régiment de Chasseurs based at Berlin operated 3 squadrons of AMX13 C90s until 1983-84, when they adopted the AMX30B.

Division type 67: 19° Groupe de Chasseurs Mécanisés en 1973

Cellule	M 56 PC S470	M 56 S470 chef de section	M 56 CAFL 38 rang	M 56 S470 échelon	M 56 S470 cargo SS11	M 56 sanitaire	M 55	AMX 13/90	AMX13/75 TCA	AMX 13/75 TCM
Compagnie de Commandement et des Services										
Section de commandement	2									
Section de dépannage							2			
Section sanitaire						2				
TOTAL	2					2	2			
1° Compagnie										
Section de commandement	1			1						
1° section de combat		1	2							
2° section de combat		1	2							
3° section de combat		1	2							
4° section de combat		1	2							
TOTAL	1	4	8	1						
2° Escadron										
Peloton de commandement	1			1				1		
1° peloton								3		
2° peloton								3		
3° peloton								3		
4° peloton								3		
Peloton SS11 TCA					1				4	
TOTAL	1			1	1			13	4	

3° Compagnie							
Section de commandement	1				1		
1° section de combat		1	2				
2° section de combat		1	2				
3° section de combat		1	2				
4° section de combat		1	2				
TOTAL	1	4	8		1		
4° Escadron							
Peloton de commandement	1				1		
1° peloton				3			
2° peloton				3			
3° peloton				3			
4° peloton				3			
Peloton SS11 TCM						1	4
TOTAL	1			13	1	2	4
TOTAL RÉGIMENTAIRE	6	8	16	26	2	2	4

Dans la division 1967, l'infanterie mécanisée est constituée de Régiments d'Infanterie Mécanisée et de Groupes de Chasseurs Mécanisés, on a donc des RI Méca ainsi que des GCM.

French Army mechanized infantry regiments in West Germany, to replace AMX13 C90s and AMX13 SS11s. The logistic advantages of diesel standardization and of the AMX30's long range firepower were embraced. The only disadvantage was that AMX13 trained crews found the AMX30 much harder to manoeuvre in confined spaces and some property damage occurred as tanks moved through village streets. Road use was consequently reduced. The regimental system employed in the mechanized infantry changed in 1984 when the mechanized infantry units in metropolitan France were still equipped with the AMX13 C90 and AMX13 SS11. The new Division 1984 system fundamentally changed regimental and squadron structures, in both the mechanized infantry and in the ABC. This changed the tactical doctrine of how the remaining AMX13s were employed in the mechanized infantry which was unwelcome in the units concerned. The Division 1984 mechanized infantry regiment only employed a single tank squadron, halving the number of tanks in a mechanized regiment, in favour of the inclusion of an additional company of AMX10P mounted infantry. The new squadron included seventeen tanks in four platoons of four vehicles and a command tank. One result was that in August 1984 surplus mechanized infantry tank crewmen in West Germany were sent to units back in France where they were expected to return to AMX13 C90s. In a short service conscript army this usually involved complete retraining to operate the older vehicles. The units in France took another 18 months to receive their own full complement of AMX30s because of the enlargement of many armoured regiments to the RC70 pattern. During this period the AMX13 C90 and AMX30B served alongside each other in the same squadrons – an unsatisfactory combination which strained logistics and regimental workshops, and caused much frustration.

The AMX13 SS11 was the last of Mle 51 conversions to remain in service in the mechanized infantry, largely due to delays into getting the VAB HOT into service. In the middle of the 1980s (when the AMX13 SS11 was withdrawn from the two mechanised infantry regiments in each *Division Blindée* as the AMX30B arrived) the redundant AMX13 SS11s were used to form antitank missile companies of sixteen tanks commanded at divisional level. These were replaced by the VAB HOT in 1989 and the AMX13 squadron at Djibouti remained the last AMX13 gun tanks in French service.

Gendarmerie Mobile:

The AMX13 Mle 51 also served in the *1er Groupement Blindé de Gendarmerie Mobile* (based at Satory) on internal security duties. It replaced the old M4A1 Shermans that had famously deployed into Paris during the ill-fated 'Generals Putsch' of 1961. The unit was composed of two squadrons of AMX13 Mle 51s, a squadron of M8 armoured cars, a Sherman M4A3 (105mm) Dozer and thirteen halftracks. The *1er GBGM* operated a total of thirty-six stock AMX13 Mle 51s from 1962 until 1983, all of which retained the CN-75-50 gun, and none of which received the army's infrared equipment upgrade. In 1972 the *1er GBGM* received its first thirteen VTT Mle 56s to replace the old halftracks. The *Gendarmerie* was eventually issued thirty-three VTT Mle 56 APCs fitted with the CAFL 38 machine-gun turret and infrared driving lights, which remained on strength until 1998. These vehicles were supported by a single *Char de Dépannage* Mle 55 issued in 1964 which was unique in that it's A-frame jib was modified to lift both AML and AMX13 turrets. This vehicle remained in service until the VTT Mle 56s were retired.

The Training Establishment:

The substantial training establishment that supported the AMX13 equipped units in metropolitan France instructed their crewmen into the early 1990s. The *École d'Application de l'Arme Blindée Cavalerie* (or EAABC) at Saumur included one or more training squadrons of Mle 51s from the early 1950s until 1967, and a squadron of AMX13 C90s until 1976. The large base at Mailly included several training establishments that employed the AMX13. The *Centre de Tir des Engins Blindés* (or CTEB) operated a training squadron of Mle 51s which converted to AMX13 C90s in the late 1960s, and continued until it moved to the new gunnery and tactical training base at Canjuers in 1973. Two subordinate training establishments that operated under the CTEB umbrella were the *Centre d'Instruction Missiles* (or CIM) and the *Centre de Perfectionnement de la Cavalerie et d'Instruction au Tir/Arme Blindée Cavalerie* (or CPCIT/ABC) which had a further training squadron for gunnery training.

In July 1964 the *11er Régiment de Cuirassiers* became one of the armoured corps' training regiments at the Carpiagne CIABC (*Centre d'Instruction de l'Arme Blindée Cavalerie*). Because of its nature as a training unit, it soon employed a wide range of AFVs and the AMX13 series

The last 'original' Mle 51s in regular service in France were operated by the 1er GBGM, an internal security group of the French National *Gendarmerie*. This picture was taken at the Quartier Delpal at Satory, near Versailles, in May 1968. Unlike the army's AMX13s, the GBGM's were never upgraded with the CN-90-F3. (*Collection Salle d'Honneur du GBGM*)

The 1er GBGM had access to the Satory training tracks for driver training, where this Mle 51 was photographed in 1969. Most of the GBGM's Mle 51s were Type 2B chassis vehicles, without infrared equipment. (*Collection Salle d'Honneur du GBGM*)

The 1er GBGM was employed regularly for honorary duties. This parade at the Quartier Delpal was photographed in 1970. Note that the Mle 51s have the original type of turret joint seals fitted. (*Collection Salle d'Honneur du GBGM*)

These Mle 51s were photographed during training on the Zone Technique de Satory in 1971. Note some of the incremental improvements fitted to these tanks like the driver's splash boards. (*Collection Salle d'Honneur du GBGM*)

The turret roof of the Mle 51s included a commander's cupola with its characteristic domed lid and eight episcopes, the gunner's position with its two fixed periscopes, grab bars and numerous weld lines. The FL10 turret was fabricated from cast and welded sections. (*Collection Salle d'Honneur du GBGM*)

In 1971 the 1er GBGM's Mle 51s received the later style bellows-type turret seals in time for the Bastille Day Parade in Paris. The 1e GBGM's crews are seen passing before the Presidential dais. (*Collection Salle d'Honneur du GBGM*)

The 1er GBGM also participated in the 1972 *14 Juillet* parade in Paris. Most mechanised infantry regiments' Mle 51s had then been converted into AMX13 C90s and the remainder into AMX13 SS11s. As most of the earliest Mle 51s had been converted into AMX-U.S. or sold these were some of the last Mle 51s in their original configuration in France. (*Collection Salle d'Honneur du GBGM*)

made up a shrinking fraction of its armoured vehicle holdings after the AMX30 series was introduced. Nonetheless, the AMX13 Mle 51 and AMX13 C90 remained on strength until 1986 to assure the mechanized infantry's training needs.

On 1 August 1976 the *1e Régiment de Chasseurs* became a gunnery training regiment at the newly created Canjuers CPCIT (*Centre de Perfectionnement de la Cavalerie et d'Instruction au Tir*). Alongside other AFV types, it retained the AMX13 C90 on strength until 1986 when the type was withdrawn from the mechanised infantry. The AMX13 SS11 remained in service for training with the regiment until 1989 when it was superseded as an antitank vehicle by the VAB HOT in the divisional antitank companies. In West Germany the ABC's training establishments included 2 AMX13 crew training squadrons based at the *Centre d'Instruction Des Blindés* (or CIDB) at Trier-Feyen. After the CIDB transferred to Carpiagne in 1968, a single squadron of AMX13 C90s remained in Trier with the mechanized infantry's *Centre de Pilotage et de Tir* (or CPT) manned by staff detached from the 8th *Groupe de Chasseurs Mécanisés*. After 1980 the CPT's staffing role was taken over by the corps of engineers.

Chapter Twelve

Derivatives of the AMX13

After the construction of prototype hulls in 1949 the AMX chassis was intended to serve as the basis for a family of armoured vehicles. The army and DEFA's engineers had rigorously studied German and American design methods for families of vehicles and intended to make the most of standard chassis types in the light and medium categories. The AMX hull's front-engine layout and existing dimensions offered the rear half of the chassis to applications like a 105mm self-propelled gun or an armoured personnel carrier. The expectation that the AMX tank hull would be built in volume also went some way towards controlling unit costs for which the French also hoped to secure some US funding contribution. Procurement costs, however, were borne by the French taxpayer after 1955 because the US administration did not recognize the necessity to fund production of a family of vehicles. The AMX chassis was also the basis for many experimental versions but only those selected for production are described below.

OB 105 Mle 50 AU Self-Propelled Gun:
The first major production derivative based on the AMX13 chassis was a light 105mm self-propelled howitzer known as the *Obusier de 105 Mle 1950 sur affût automoteur* (or by the simpler abbreviation OB 105 Mle 50 AU). This artillery system was built in prototype form in 1948 on an early experimental AMX chassis. The OB 105 50 105mm gun was mounted in an armoured casemate with an armoured roof; it had an elevation of -4 to 66 degrees and a 37 degree traverse. The howitzer's mounting was quite large for the small size of the chassis and was modified to occupy a smaller footprint in the fighting compartment during development. The front-engine layout of the AMX13 hull proved ideal for a self-propelled field gun. Ammunition stowage of 54 rounds and a six-man crew were carried in the version adopted by the French artillery. When ordered in 1950 the 16.5-tonne OB 105 Mle 50 AU was the first tank-based self-propelled gun adopted by the French Army which gave it high priority despite not being funded by American aid.[27]

Series production of the OB 105 Mle 50 AU was consequently delayed and unit tests began in summer 1954 with the *8e Régiment d'Artillerie*. In all 329 units were manufactured on the type 2C chassis from July 1954. The OB 105 Mle 50 AU was also sold to Israel, Morocco and to West Germany (in trial quantities). These simple and effective vehicles remained in French artillery service for over three decades but the 105mm calibre was superseded as divisional artillery by the 155mm gun from 1968 onwards. This signalled the replacement of the OB 105 Mle 50 AUs by the *Canon 155 Automouvante F3* and eventually by the Au F1. The parallel development of a turreted version of the 105mm self-propelled gun on the AMX chassis was undertaken from 1952 by the *Atelier de Bourges* with unrealized hopes of a French order. This version had a slightly improved gun (with the barrel length extended from 23 to 30 calibres) capable of firing a wider variety of 105mm rounds to a slightly longer range. It was never successfully marketed excepting a small run of four vehicles built in 1960 for Switzerland and at least one prototype evaluated by the French artillery. The Netherlands and Indonesia bought an updated version of the OB 105 Mle 50 AU with the 30 calibre 105mm gun in the early 1960s. Export versions of the OB 105 Mle 50 AU have received the English designation 'AMX 105 Mk.61' (or simply 'AMX Mk.61').[28]

AMX13 Ml 1955 Char de Dépannage:

A recovery variant of the AMX13 was planned from the early 1950s, but because wartime recovery vehicles were available the prototype did not appear until 1954 and was not ordered until 1955. Its design incorporated a fixed superstructure with a winch and an A-frame permitting the lifting of heavy assemblies. The recovery vehicle was variously designated "*Char de Dépannage AMX*", "*Char de Dépannage AMX M. 55*" or "*Char de Dépannage AMX Mle 55*" in official army technical documents. To the average cavalryman and in the mechanized infantry it was often simply referred to as "the CD" or "the M55". Production began at AMX in 1957 and 2 distinct production versions existed for the *Char de Dépannage*, early vehicles sharing features with the Type 2B chassis and late vehicles sharing features with the 2D chassis. The recovery vehicle was purchased by nearly every army that employed AMX13s, and some remain in service today.[29]

The first prototype of the OB 105 AU at Bourges during the firing tests on 28 July 1950. Note the hull form and the use of the 6 spoked idler. (*Photo S.C.A. / Peter Lau Collection*)

A French Army OB 105 Mle 50 AU manoeuvring in the Mailly-le-Camp training ground in April 1959. (*Peter Lau Collection*)

The OB 105 Mle 50 AU was the French artillery's most modern weapon from 1954 until 1967 when the AM F3 began to replace it in the Division 1967's order of battle. The process was not complete until the late 1970s; this OB 105 Mle 50 AU of the *32e Régiment d'Artillerie* was photographed in 1976 at Suippes during a training exercise. (*Denis Verdier*)

The little OB 105 Mle 50 AU took much of its inspiration from the German Wespe and, when first introduced it was an ideal field artillery weapon for the DMR experiment of the mid-1950s. It packed the same kind of firepower as an M7 Priest on a lighter and more manoeuvrable chassis. (*Denis Verdier*)

One of the OB 105 Mle 50 AU's convenient features was the large rear door that could be opened to quickly replenish ammunition or for ventilation. The small size of the fixed casemate belied its crew of 6 men and an ability to carry over 50 rounds of ammunition. (*Denis Verdier*)

The interior of the OB 105 Mle 50 AU's casemate was dominated by the breech of its 105mm gun. The large cut-out in the armoured roof allows the periscopic sight to traverse. (*Denis Verdier*)

An OB 105 Mle 50 AU and crewmen of the 32e RA at Suippes in 1977. The AA-52 machinegun normally mounted on the commander's cupola pintle is fitted and some details of the casemate roof are also visible. (*Denis Verdier*)

The OB 105 Mle 50 AU was already being replaced in the Division 1977 because the 155mm artillery calibre was far more effective. After 1985 a large number were employed as hard targets. The closely related Mk.61 remains in use in Indonesia to the present day. (*Denis Verdier*)

The OB 105 Mle 50 AU was withdrawn from French service during 1985. This very complete example (minus its tools) was preserved at the 40e RA's base with several other retired artillery pieces. The 3-colour camouflage scheme is probably erroneous and the *numéro d'immatriculation* has disappeared, but this would have been the exterior of the OB 105 Mle 50 had it remained in French service until the end of the Cold War (*Pierre Delattre*)

The OB 105-50 105mm gun could elevate to + 70 degrees and could also be clamped into a folding gun crutch when necessary to avoid damage to the elevation gear. (*Pierre Delattre*)

An OB 015 Mle 50 AU, wearing typical markings worn by the type, awaiting disposal at the end of the Cold War. (*Jerome Hadacek*)

Switzerland almost standardized the turreted OB 105 AU self-propelled gun. This preserved example included late production features like the cast pattern idler from the Series 2D, but had a wider hull than in the light tank versions. (*Massimo Fotti*)

A front view of the turreted OB 105 AU preserved at Saumur. France adopted the AM F3 (a much less sophisticated vehicle) whilst awaiting the very modern turreted AU F1 155mm GCT which only entered service in 1979. (*Philippe Besson*)

AMX13 Poseur de Pont:

The Indochina war gave the *Corps du Génie* an impetus to develop modern bridging systems to replace the wartime era equipment. While French bridging doctrine oriented itself towards the wheeled bridging amphibian vehicle in the 1950s, the AMX13 chassis was selected to carry a short span scissors type bridge for use with light mechanized forces. The *AMX Poseur de Pont F1* (PP F1) bridge layer designed in 1957 provided divisional engineers with a vehicle that could launch a 14m scissors bridge in under ten minutes. Because the *Génie* preferred wheeled amphibian *engins de franchissement* over tracked bridge layers the production PP F1 was delayed for nearly a decade. Fully loaded, the AMX13 PP F1 weighed 19 tonnes and was capable of laying two different types of F1 25 tonne portable bridge (*Travure Simple* and the joinable *Travure Couplable*, each suitable to span a 12 m gap). A 50 tonne bridge was also designed. In all forty-five bridge layer *AMX13 Poseur de Pont (PP) F1s* were built at AMX on the Type E chassis from 1966 for the French Army (with ninety bridges built by Coder of Marseilles). The first of these entered service in 1968, and they served until the end of the Cold War. A smaller number of AMX *Poseur de Pont F1s* were built at AMX for export customers as orders were received for other AMX13 type vehicles.[30]

An overhead view of a CD Mle 55 manufactured in the late 1950s before the Type D chassis was adopted for the VTT Mle 56, the last batches of Mle 51 tanks and for the Mle 58. The CD Mle 55 was a long-lived and well-engineered light recovery vehicle. (*Thomas Seignon*)

This Char de Depannage Mle 55 was photographed in service with the *35e Régiment d'Infanterie Mécanisé* in 1964. The mechanised infantry regiments received the CD Mle 55 along with its new VTT Mle 56s from 1960. This is a late pattern CD Mle 55, built to a standard that incorporated features common to the Type 2D chassis. Many exported CD Mle 55s resemble this configuration. (*Collection Daniel Hecket*)

The CD Mle 55 was quite agile and speedy across country and equipped with a winch and folding A-frame jib. It proved adequate for most field recovery tasks associated with the AMX13 and its derivatives. (*Collection Daniel Hecket*)

The photo shows both the driver's position and the arrangement of the front of the CD Mle 55's hull. Most of the differences between the early and late production CD Mle 55s were in their electrical systems and suspensions. (*Collection Daniel Hecket*)

Climbing out of a hollow at Mourmelon in 1964, this DC Mle 55 of the 35e RI shows the crew positions in the vehicle superstructure, rear spades and the folded A-frame jib. (*Collection Daniel Hecket*)

This CD Mle 55 was assigned to the 1e GBGM and was photographed at Satory in 1969. It was from the first production series, and it went on to be the last CD Mle 55 in service in France. (*Collection Salle d'Honneur du GBGM*)

The jib crane raised halfway. The CD Mle 55 was issued with the original pattern steel tracks. (*Collection Salle d'Honneur du GBGM*)

Rear view of the same vehicle in 1974, after the rubber padded tracks had been universally adopted for road use. The spades, tow bars and the towing pintle on the rear plate are visible. (*Collection Salle d'Honneur du GBGM*)

The CD Mle 55 was often a star in regimental open day displays. This recovery team from the *150e Régiment d'Infanterie* deploys this Mle 55's jib crane in dramatic style in 1983. (*Guy Gibeau*)

The conclusion of such demonstrations was often the removal of an AMX13's turret, a feat of strength well within the CD Mle 55's capabilities. (*Guy Gibeau*)

AMX VTT Mle 56 and Derivatives:

The VTT Mle 56 armoured personnel carrier was built in greater numbers than the Mle 51 itself and was based on a lengthened AMX13 Type 2D type chassis. The French army sought a dedicated armoured personnel carrier (or APC) from 1945 but funding problems caused the wartime halftrack to be retained into the 1960s. The halftrack lacked an enclosed fighting compartment and the cross country performance expected in the next generation of tanks. A first AMX based 12-man carrier proposed in 1948 was rejected by the infantry. Ultimately designs from eight engineering firms were evaluated as potential APC candidates by the French infantry and were in some cases built and tested, with Hotchkiss products consistently in the forefront. As it wavered between six and nine man carriers the army did not confirm a satisfactory APC until 1955. The Hotchkiss 6-man carrier was very nearly adopted by the French infantry branch (and it secured a sizeable West German order) but ultimately the general staff insisted on the adoption of the AMX13 derivative which commenced trials in 1956.

The AMX carrier was standardized as the TT CH Mle56 (*Transport de Troupes Chenillé Modèle 1956* or troop carrier, tracked, model 1956) but it was more commonly known as the

This picture was taken during the post-exercise cleaning and maintenance of an AMX13 PP F1 operated by the 9e RG in 1976. Without the bridge fitted, the basic hull and superstructure can be clearly seen. The *Poseur de Pont* was developed in the late 1950s but was not produced and issued until 1967. The hulls consequently had many late features shared with the Type 2D chassis. (*Michel Huhardeaux*)

The bridge was launched from the rear of the vehicle and when loaded it rested on a stout support beam anchored to the hull front on either side of the front plate. This vehicle is being cleaned free from the heavy burden of its *travure*. The *code de wagonnage* railway marking is visible on the tool bin on the left side of the photos. (*Michel Huhardeaux*)

With a crewman observing on the roof of the superstructure, the *Poseur de Pont* prepares to recover its bridge, possibly during a demonstration to the public. The hydraulic cylinders are at full extension and the riveted fulcrum and launch supports can be seen. (*Michel Huhardeaux*)

The *Heiteren*, minus its bridge, manoeuvres with crewmen braced on the superstructure. (*Michel Huhardeaux*)

The *Heiteren* lays a bridge – seen here at partial extension. (*Michel Huhardeaux*)

The *Poseur de Pont F1* could bridge a relatively small gap but allowed engineer units to get a 25 tonne bridge into use in a matter of minutes. (*Michel Huhardeaux*)

During bridge laying the PP F1's driver faced the opposite way. The actual bridge deployment was conducted from the superstructure by the commander and operator. (*Michel Huhardeaux*)

The loaded *Poseur de Pont F1* was the heaviest member of the AMX13 family. The photo shows a number of bridges stocked for loading on any of the 4 PP F1s that would have been on the regiment's war establishment. (*Michel Huhardeaux*)

The unloaded the *Poseur de Pont* was responsive and speedy but when loaded it was top heavy and had to be handled carefully on uneven ground. The PP F1 remains in service in some armies to this day. (*Michel Huhardeaux*)

VTT Mle 56 (*Vehicule Transport de Troupes Modèle 1956*). The French VTTs were delivered from 1960, armed originally with the CAFL 38 7.5mm machine gun turret and with the S470 cupola mounting a 12.7mm heavy machine gun in later batches. A 73mm LRAC (*Lance Roquette AntiChar*) antitank rocket launcher was carried inside to protect the infantry section from enemy armour. The VTT Mle 56 gave the mechanised infantry a far more capable weapon than the old halftracks but it was not amphibious. Cost considerations limited delivery to about 200 vehicles per year. The Type 1959 mechanised infantry regiment was equipped with three companies of VTTs, a reconnaissance company in Hotchkiss Jeeps and a command and support company. This organisation changed when the mechanised infantry changed to the Type 1967 regimental structures. The *Arme Blindée Cavalerie* also employed the VTT Mle 56 in the *régiment de chars de bataille* in the *Division 1959*, and subsequently under the *Division 1967* and *Division 1977* structures in the RC54 type battle tank regiment and in cavalry units that retained the AMX13 C90.

The VTT Mle 56 design was adequately armoured and carried a practical number of troops. Its passengers were capable of firing from the vehicle, but its main drawbacks were tied to the use of an existing tank chassis as the basis for the design. In 1968 (well before the BMPs deployed in the 1973 Arab-Israeli war shocked the western armies into designing the IFVs of the 1970s and 1980s) Richard Ogorkiewicz summed up the design as follows:

> The French Army produced an original design which represented the first attempt at a tracked armoured carrier that was not merely a 'battle taxi' but a vehicle from which the infantry could fight on the move... It enjoys several logistical advantages but the rationalization with other vehicles restricted the freedom of action of its designers. This is particularly evident in the retention, almost unchanged, of the front section of the AMX 13 hull with its side-by-side engine and driving compartments. As a result, the front end of the AMX-VTT is not as good as it might be both from the point of view of compactness and of ballistic protection.[31]

The main mechanical drawback in comparison to the M113A1 was the VTT Mle 56's retention of the SOFAM petrol engine and its lack of amphibious capabilities. Its main competitor in the armoured personnel carrier market was the M113, a vehicle produced in far larger quantity with a lower unit cost. The AMX10P mechanized infantry fighting vehicle supplemented and eventually replaced the VTT Mle 56 in the mechanised infantry and in the *Arme Blindée Cavalerie*'s from 1973 onwards. The VTT Mle 56 was upgraded to supplement the slow annual production of the AMX10P. France had neither the funds nor the production capacity to replace all of the VTT Mle 56s with AMX10Ps in the mid-1970s. The next best option was to fit a manually traversed 1-man version of the AMX10P's TH20 TOUCAN turret (designated the *tourelleau T20-13* or *tourelleau T20-13*) to the VTT Mle 56.

The T20-13 turret was armed with a GIAT 20mm F2 cannon and a co-axial 7.62mm AA-52 machinegun, but it could not be simply fitted to the existing VTT Mle 56s armed with the CAFL 38 and S470 machine gun cupolas in regimental workshops. Conversion required a factory rebuild to fit the turret and race, accommodate the ammunitions supply and update the interior stowage arrangements. Most notably, the converted vehicle's rear bench seats were more widely spaced to accommodate the 630 rounds of boxed 20mm ammunition,

The CAFL 38 turret was standard on the first VTT Mle 56s ordered for the French infantry; it was equipped with the MAC31 7.5mm machinegun for French orders. (*Pierre Delattre*)

The cast CAFL 38 turret allowed the vehicle crew to put down suppressive fire while the infantry dismounted or to engage enemies caught in the open. (*Pierre Delattre*)

This VTT Mle 56 was operated by the 1e GBGM and photographed in 1972 on the Satory training area. (*Collection Salle d'Honneur du GBGM*)

The VTT Mle 56 replaced the US Halftrack used for many years in the French infantry. It introduced a modified suspension also adopted on the Mle51 Type 2D and Mle 58 chassis. This 1e GBMG VTT Mle 56 was photographed at Satory in 1974. (*Collection Salle d'Honneur du GBGM*)

A GBGM VTT Mle 56 with CAFL38 turret photographed on the Rambouillet base area in December 1978 in snowy conditions. (*Collection Salle d'Honneur du GBGM*)

The VTT Mle 56, especially in the French mechanised infantry, was extensively modified in the mid-1970s to conform to the same standard of armament as the AMX10P. The GBGM retained original VTT Mle 56s right up to the end of the Cold War. (*Collection Salle d'Honneur du GBGM*)

In 1980 these 1e GBGM VTT 1956s were photographed on the Satory training area. Many of their *Gendarme* crews had already served on armour during national service. Some of them spent their entire careers specialising in internal security; it was often from this pool of specialists that the presidential drivers and escorts were selected for public events where VIP security was of special concern. (*Collection Salle d'Honneur du GBGM*)

In the *Arme Blindée Cavalerie* the VTT Mle 56 was employed as a command vehicle in all M47 squadrons. The group seen here include a squadron command vehicle crew and squadron commander from the *2e Régiment de Cuirassiers* in the early 1970s. This VTT is equipped with the S470 cupola, normally fitted with a 12.7mm heavy machine gun for local defence. (*Jean Beaudouin*)

This VTT Mle 56 was also photographed serving in the command role in the 18e Régiment de Dragons in the 1970s. It is fitted with the S470 cupola. The AMX10P in the background was a rather more sophisticated vehicle which served in the mechanised infantry and also in the *Arme Blindée Cavalerie*'s AMX30 regiments. (*Thomas Seignon*)

The VTT Mle 56 T20-13 could be used in an air defence role and collective firing was practised. These vehicles from the 30e GC were photographed on the ranges at Suippes in 1986. (*Collection Jean Ancher*)

A photo taken on the Suippes ranges in November 1986 showing a VTT Mle 56 T20-13 of the 30e GC in a muddy fire position with the rear doors open. (*Collection Jean Ancher*)

The addition of the T20-13 turret did not affect the VTT Mle 56's cross country performance. This VTT Mle 56 T20-13 was photographed during a cross country performance demonstration for men of the 30e GC in 1982 (*Collection Jean Ancher*)

An early *AMX13 Véhicule de Transport de Troupes Modèle 56* with the CAFL38 turret of the *46e Régiment d'Infanterie*, serving in Berlin in the early 1960s. (*J.J. Montegnies*)

This VTT SAN photographed at Mailly belonged to the headquarters ECL of the *1e Régiment de Cuirassiers* in 1978, as can be seen by the *tour d'Auvergne* badge of the *Maréchal* de Turenne who founded the regiment. The 1e RC was a Patton regiment in the Division 1959 and was equipped with the AMX30B in the late 1960s. Like all armoured regiments they employed the AMX13 SS11 alongside the Patton and the VTT in several guises, right up to the 1980s. (*Thomas Seignon*)

This VTT SAN was one of the very first built around 1960. The main external identifiers (besides the large red crosses common to most ambulance vehicles) were the total absence of armament and the AMX13 Mle 51-type commander's cupola. The VTT SAN was progressively replaced as an ambulance by the wheeled VAB SAN in the 1980s, but some remained in service until the end of the Cold War. (*Thomas Seignon*)

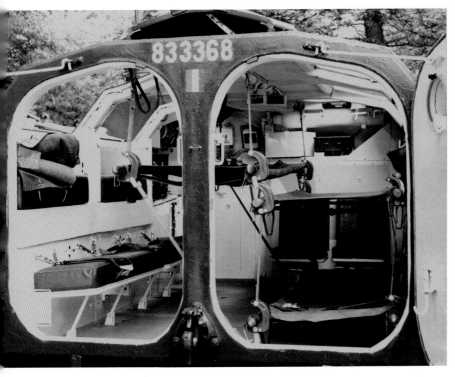

The modular style of interior that was fitted to the VTT SAN allowed several configurations for the transport of wounded soldiers. The most common was the mixed 4 sitting and 2 lying on stretchers arrangement visible here. A maximum of 4 stretchers could be carried. (*Thomas Seignon*)

In contrast we can see the interior of the infantry compartment at the rear of the VTT Mle 56, in this case a VTT Mle 56 T20-13. The infantrymen sat back to back, and were provided with roof hatches and firing ports in the hull sides. (*Marcel Toulon*)

The infantry group carried by a VTT included two AA-52 general purpose machinegun teams, two LRAC rocket launchers, and eight riflemen. These are infantrymen of the *5e Régiment d'Infanterie* seen dismounting from a VTT Mle 56 T20-13 during a display in 1979. (*Marcel Toulon*)

Arpajon, a VTT Mle 56 T20-13 of the *Régiment de Marche du Tchad*, showing the bulk of its 20mm gun turret in 1980. (*Marcel Toulon*)

Laid out on the spare road wheel, a belt of 20mm ammunition. The VTT Mle 56 T20-13 packed an impressive punch. (*Marcel Toulon*)

The rear of the turret; showing how the weapon itself was mounted outside of the vehicle's armour envelope. On the VTT Mle 56 T20-13 this turret was traversed by hand and was operated by one man. The automatic cannon could be elevated to high angles for engaging helicopters. (*Marcel Toulon*)

The front of the 20mm turret installation with the gun at high elevation. (*Marcel Toulon*)

which reduced the infantry passengers' leg room. At the same time the interior stowage was altered to accept the LRAC 89mm antitank rocket launcher. The turret dual type feed system held 170 rounds (100 rounds of high explosive and 70 of armour piercing which could penetrate 20mm of armour at 1000 metres). The weapon had a range of 1000m-1300m in a ground role and of 1500m against aerial targets.[32]

Conversions and issue of the VTT Mle 56 T20-13 to the mechanized infantry began in 1973 (normally with 27 vehicles per unit), coinciding roughly with the AMX10P's entry into service. A total of 432 conversions were completed as re-equipment with the AMX10P freed up available batches of VTT Mle 56s, including 13 vehicles for the training unit (EAI) based at Garrigues. The first two units to field the new VTT Mle 56 T20-13 were the *24e Groupe de Chasseurs Mécanisés* in late 1973, followed by the *19e Groupe de Chasseurs Mécanisés* at the beginning of 1974. Cavalry units still equipped with the AMX13 C90 also received 27 VTT Mle 56 T20-13s in place of 24 VTT Mle 56s equipped with the older machine gun turrets in the same year. By the time the Division 1977 was fully implemented, 11 mechanized infantry units and 7 cavalry units had received the VTT Mle 56 T20-13 as partial equipment. The vehicle serial on the rebuilt VTTs started with the digits 638 or 648.

The AMX13 C90 and VTT Mle 56 T20-13 were gradually replaced in the cavalry with the AMX30B and AMX10P as the Division 1977 system was implemented, but the older AMX13 based vehicles remained in some units until the early 1980s (generally units in France kept the VTT Mle 56 until units in West Germany received their full quota of the amphibious AMX10P). After 1976 128 redundant VTT Mle 56 T20-13s were modified to carry Milan missile teams. Each mechanized infantry regiment received two sections of four VTT Mle 56 T20-13 Milan, even the *1er Groupe de Chasseurs Mécanisés,* who had been the first unit to convert to the amphibious AMX10P. The VTT Mle 56 T20-13 and Milan vehicles served into the 1980s and many of the updated VTT Mle 56s were sold on to other armies after the Cold War.

The VTT Mle 56 was used as the basis for the *Vehicule Sanitaire* (ambulance version which first entered service in 1959), VTT *Cargo* (which was used to carry missiles for the AMX13 SS-11 and other stores), VTT *Poste de Commandement* (command vehicle), VTT *Porte Mortier* (mortar carrier built only for export orders), VTT RATAC (Artillery Acquisition Radar), VTT SA (*Soutien d'Artillerie*), the VTT Milan equipped with Milan ATGMs (introduced in 1976) and the VCG (*Véhicule de Combat du Genie*). The VCG was one of the last VTT versions purpose built for the French Army; sixty-seven were ordered in 1962. It was fitted with a winch, dozer blade and could carry a full combat engineers section. Production was delayed until 1967 due to funding shortfalls and the VCG was first issued to troops in 1969. It served for over twenty years alongside the PP Flas the maid of all work in the divisional engineers' regiments. The designation AMX13 VCI (for *Véhicule de Combat d'Infanterie*) was used by DEFA, DTAT and GIAT for newly built, foreign licence-built or second-hand export versions of the VTT Mle 56. Many VCIs exported with the CAFL38 turret were equipped with 7.62mm machineguns.[33]

Also seen at the CPT at Trier in 1977, this VCG (*Véhicule de Combat du Génie*) is being used to qualify a driver from the *13e Régiment de Génie*. The staffing of the CPT at Trier, founded in 1955 by the *ABC* and taken over by the infantry in the 1960s, was in turn later taken over by the engineers who employed the VCG into the 1990s. (*Guy Gibeau*)

The VCG seen here was photographed in 1976 in eastern France and belonged to the *9e Régiment du Génie*, based at Neuf Brisach in France. Photos of the VCG and Poseur de Pont in use are rare and the authors thank Michel Huhardeaux for allowing us to use these. (*Michel Huhardeaux*)

The VCG was based on the VTT Mle 56 and was intended for use as a maid of all work for the combat engineer regiments attached to each armoured division. It featured a front mounted dozer blade for light earth moving tasks, such as preparing crossing points or scraping out firing positions. (*Michel Huhardeaux*)

The VCG *Andlau* is fitted with the older fabricated plate idler seen on early Mle 51s – by all appearances a standard practice. The utility trailer was employed to carry a whole range of supplies essential for battlefield demolition, area denial operations, or for construction tasks. (*Michel Huhardeaux*)

The VCG was equipped with the S470 cupola as standard, seen here without its 12.7mm machinegun mounted. (*Michel Huhardeaux*)

After operations on the training ground, it was standard practice in all arms to clean the vehicles with high pressure hoses. This VTT Mle 56 *Fronholz* is on strength of the *9e Régiment du Génie*. (*Michel Huhardeaux*)

The VCG was also equipped with a front mounted winch and an A Frame which could be configured for lifting tasks and for clearing obstacles from roadways. (*Michel Huhardeaux*)

The VCG, like the VTT Mle 56, was built on a lengthened Type 2D chassis. This view gives some idea of the layout of the roof hatches, which could be opened for ventilation in rear areas or could be used by its passengers to fire from the vehicle. (*Michel Huhardeaux*)

This VCG was photographed in the dry summer of 1976 on the 9e RG's base area. (*Michel Huhardeaux*)

CN 155 F3 Am or AM F3:

The French artillery had studied the adoption of a 155mm gunned SPG since evaluating the 150mm gunned German Hummel in 1945. The design of a turreted 155mm self-propelled gun was pursued in the 1950s without success. The AMX based 155mm self-propelled gun began development in 1957 and the prototype was first demonstrated in 1964. It mounted an OB 155 Mle 50 155mm gun with a barrel extended to 30 calibres. A range of 20 km was possible firing the OB Mle 56 hollow base shell or 17 km firing older Mle 50 rounds. Delays in converting the French divisional artillery to 155mm calibre were caused by experimentation in munition delivered antitank mine programmes. The trend towards the adoption of the 155mm as the divisional artillery was followed throughout NATO at the same time. In France the simplest means of getting a 155mm divisional self-propelled gun into service prevailed after years of indecision.

The *Canon Automouvante 155mm F3* (AM F3) consisted of the gun mounting and stub trail of a CN 155 Mle 50 155mm gun fixed into the rear of a modified AMX13 chassis. This gun was no more advanced than the old M40 self-propelled 155mm guns of 1945, but it had the advantage of weighing 17.5 tonnes. The hull featured a modified suspension without the rear idlers and with a different track tensioning system. The disadvantages of such a small hull were that no ammunition could be carried on board and that the complete gun crew could not travel with the piece. Only the gun commander and driver travelled on the vehicle and no NBC protection was provided. As a result, each AM F3 was accompanied by a VTT modified to carry twenty-five rounds of 155mm ammunition and the remaining six members of the gun crew (in addition to the vehicle driver). The weapon proved quick to bring into battery and a well-trained crew could fire as many as six rounds per minute. In late 1966 the first 150 AM F3s were ordered for France, sufficient to arm the first ten divisional artillery regiments replacing older guns; the order was later extended to 222 guns. Production began in 1968 at Creusot-Loire. Production or reconditioning for foreign orders at the *Atelier de Roanne* was continued by GIAT after Creusot-Loire ceased to operate.[34]

A gun crew from one of the AM F3s of the *3e Régiment d'Artillerie de Marine* during a range period at Canjuers in January 1986. Each carries a FAMAS assault rifle. They have a stock of 155mm rounds ready and are waiting for the order to begin firing. (*Alain Dépré*)

A 155mm round ready on its loading tray. Each member of the gun crew had a carefully determined role in loading and firing the AM F3's gun. (*Alain Dépré*)

The smoke after fire from the *Tchad*'s 155mm gun. Note the high elevation possible with the 155mm gun mounting. (*Alain Dépré*)

With rear spades lowered and with a MIRADOP miniature Doppler fire radar fitted to the gun tube, this AM F3 is prepared to find a target's range. One MIRADOP (MIni RAdar DOPpler) was provided to each 5-gun battery. The MIRADOP and the RATAC artillery radar systems were employed with the ATILA computerized battery fire control system in French divisional artillery regiments, giving them one of the most advanced artillery battlefield information systems in the world at that time. (*Alain Dépré*)

The *Verdun* of the 3e RAMa preparing to fire during an exercise in 1986. We can see 7 of the crewmen, the loaded shell cradle installed in line with the breech and the rammer in place. To fire, the shell would be pushed into the breech followed by a bagged charge, the breech would be screwed shut, and the firing lanyard would be pulled as the crewmen brace themselves for the roar of the gun firing. (*Alain Dépré*)

This AM F3 of the 3e RAMa was photographed at Canjuers preparing to fire during an exercise in October 1986. (*Alain Dépré*)

The *Tchad* prepares to fire in the background while a surveyor completes his tasks on the firing position. Survey personnel were still essential for accurate fire with medium artillery despite the introduction of battlefield radar. (*Alain Dépré*)

An AM F3 crew preparing to fire in October 1986. The gun commander's fire plan is visible on the left of the gun breech. The gun commander and both drivers wore AFV helmets while the rest of the gun crew were attired in standard combat uniform and webbing. (*Alain Dépré*)

The *Tchad*'s crew readying the gun to fire in October 1986. (*Alain Dépré*)

The gun layer and one of the gun crew of this AM F3 photographed on rainy night in 1986 demonstrating one of the AM F3's salient drawbacks: it was a vehicle utterly bereft of crew comforts. The crew was much more vulnerable to the weather than in contemporary self-propelled guns like the M109. (*Alain Dépré*)

The gun commander and driver manoeuvre the AM F3 across the battlefield towards their next firing position. The VTT with the rest of the gun crew and 25 rounds of ammunition would be close behind. We can see the diminutive size of the AM F3. (*Alain Dépré*)

The *4e Batterie, 1e Régiment d'Artillerie* prior to departing on manoeuvres in 1981. After the AU F1 began to enter service around 1980–81, the number of AM F3 guns in each artillery regiment was increased to 20. This created a 4th battery in each artillery regiment, which permitted divisional headquarters to assign a 155mm battery to support each of the 2 armoured regiments and each of the 2 mechanised regiments. (*Denis Verdier*)

A VTT RATAC of the *1e Régiment d'Artillerie* in 1983. The VTT RATAC was based on a standard VTT Mle 56 mounting the CAFL38 turret with the battlefield artillery radar system visible on the rear of the superstructure. The RATAC system was introduced in the 1970s and soon proved extremely useful for counterbattery fire. It became the basis for establishing enemy gun positions once the ATILA system was introduced. (*Denis Verdier*)

In the early 1980s the ATILA (*Automatisation des Tirs et des Liaisons de l'Artillerie*) was fitted to the AM F3 and AU F1. The ATILA computerized battery control console was located in a box on the left rear fender of the AM F3. The ATILA system was introduced to coordinate Pluton SRBM and 155mm artillery fire at division or corps level. The ATILA system was based on regimental fire control computers fed by coordinates and corrected by the RATAC artillery radars. The regimental fire control computer sent fire plan information to each gun via a console like the one pictured. It was one of the most advanced systems of its kind and it was only replaced in the late 1990s by the much more advanced ATLAS Canon system, which served a wider range of weaponry. (*Denis Verdier*)

30mm Bitube Défense Contre Avion:

Studies for a twin 30mm AA turret on the AMX chassis began in March 1953 when the SAMM firm was tasked with the design to a general technical outline supplied by the army. By 1955 four turret designs with differing fire controls, power supplies and turret race diameters were proposed for army approval. The lightest of these designs was accepted as the basis for the production turret in order to avoid changes to the AMX chassis. Two versions of the turret were envisioned, one with a simple optical fire control system and a second with radar direction and a gunnery calculator for the fire control system. The first of these was ordered but the requirement for a large diameter turret ring nonetheless forced the adoption of a modified AMX13 chassis. Hispano-Suiza was tasked with supplying the 30mm HS 830 cannons. The turret specification was finalized in April 1956 by DEFA. An unarmoured full size model turret mounted on an AMX chassis was delivered to DEFA on in June to begin testing. Trials at Toulon in September and October 1956 resulted in the redesign of the ammunition feed system. In December the model turret was fitted to an EBR hull and tested with the modifications. American funding of 25 per cent of the development costs for the SAMM turret was agreed in 1957. In May 1958 a true prototype of the turret was delivered and received the designation SAMM S400 (and later S400A when fitted with the *Oeil Noir* radar). The hull from the turreted AMX 105mm self-propelled gun was adopted for further development of the self-propelled antiaircraft tank because of the suitability of its larger turret ring.[35]

The first production vehicles (without radar) were delivered in July 1963 as the *'Bitube de 30mm antiaérien automoteur type A'* or abbreviated to '2 x 30 AA – AU – TA'. The provision of radar for the SAMM 400 turret was revisited in 1964 with the addition of the *Oeil Noir* radar system developed by *Société Electronique Marcel Dassault* and first produced in August 1964. The commander's SAGEM 1B 1x collimator sight and analog gunnery computer were used to identify targets for the gunner who engaged them with a SAGEM 4A sight with 6x magnification. The sights were linked to the gun's elevation via pantographs. Both commander and gunner had an APX M250 sight for engaging ground targets. The radar equipped S400(A) turret was tested at Colomb-Béchar, Toulon and Biscarosse from late 1965 and through 1966. As the radar sets were added to the existing *'Bitube de 30mm antiaérien automoteur type A'* from 1967 through 1969 the designation was changed to *'Bitube de 30mm antiaérien automoteur type B'* (more commonly known as the *'AMX 13 Bitube de 30, DCA'*). All 70 production vehicles were converted by the end of 1969 although 100 SAMM 400 turrets were manufactured.[36]

The *AMX13 Bitube de 30mm Défense Contre Avion* (or DCA) was too costly to buy in larger numbers so the artillery used them as a single battery of each 3-battery divisional antiaircraft regiment. Until the Roland missile was introduced each regiment had two other batteries equipped with a mixed armament of 40mm Bofors and lighter AA weapons (M16 halftracks and towed 20mm guns). The *AMX13 Bitube de 30mm DCA* battery was organized in 3 *Sections de Tir* of 3 *AMX13 Bitubes* (with 1 *AMX13 Bitube* for the battery commander). They served until 1989 in the increasingly missile-oriented AA regiments. As self-propelled anti-aircraft vehicles they were very advanced when initially introduced but suffered both from a smaller ammunition capacity and a worse cross country performance than the Mle 51.[37]

A mud-splattered *AMX13 30mm Bitube DCA* from the *53e Régiment d'Artillerie's* self-propelled 30mm battery on manoeuvres in the Mulheim area with the *3e Division Mecanisée* in the *Forces Francaises en Allemagne*. (*J.-M. Cambier with thanks to Antoine Misner*)

Maintenance in progress on the Mulheim base area on one of the 53e Régiment d'Artillerie's *AMX13 30mm Bitube DCAs* in the 1970s. The AMX13 family required substantial front-end dismantling to replace the engine or transmission. (*J.-M. Cambier with thanks to Antoine Misner*)

The front end dismantled and the transmission is ready for removal. (J.-M. Cambier with thanks to Antoine Misner)

An *AMX13 30mm Bitube DCA* of the 53e Régiment d'Artillerie with its crew after an exercise in the 1970s. The yellow tactical marking would be replaced by the NATO tactical marking after 1977. Note how neatly the radar antennae folds into the turret bustle. (*J.-M. Cambier with thanks to Antoine Misner*)

Douai, with her crew at a display in the late 1970s. The markings are still those typically seen for artillery units prior to 1977. The radar dish is traversed rearwards for folding; the gunner's and commander's sights are visible. The main drawback with the *AMX13 30mm Bitube DCA* was its small ammunition capacity. (*Marcel Toulon*)

Rêve de Vierge is a pristine example of the *AMX13 30mm Bitube DCA* maintained at the Saumur Musée des Blindées. The *AMX13 30mm Bitube DCA* was slightly top-heavy and was one of the weightiest AMX13 variants. (*Jerome Hadacek*)

The rear of the SAMM turret was modified to accommodate the folding *Oeil Noir* radar antennae after adoption (but prior to issue) because the radar specification was added retrospectively. As a result the divisional air defence regiments only received the *AMX13 30mm Bitube DCA* in the late 1960s, and its high unit cost resulted in a small order. (*Pierre Delattre*)

While the AMX13 chassis proved too small to produce an ideal Self-Propelled Antiaircraft Gun (SPAAG), the SAMM turret was expected to be developed further and on multiple chassis. It was also evaluated on the Panhard EBR hull, and ultimately evolved into the AMX30 Bitube 30mm DCA exported to Saudi Arabia. (*J.M. Boniface*)

Chapter Thirteen

The AMX13 as an Export Success

The AMX13 sold well for three decades due to its powerful armament and reasonable price – and DEFA's marketing efforts. Nearly half of all AMX13 series vehicles were produced for foreign orders and some vehicles retired from French service were sold abroad. Export of the original Mle 51 was given high priority in the 1950s because it stimulated a significant part of the heavy industry sector. The AMX13 had a better antitank performance than the M41 Walker Bulldog or PT-76; its main market competitors in the 1950s were the heavier British Centurion and the US M47.

DEFA's efforts to export the AMX13 caused some friction with the US because the MDAA funding agreement committed France to equip her own forces first. The Americans wanted to support strategic allies to rearm quickly but not to enable those allies to sell arms for profit. The French, meanwhile, did not want their hands tied and made a point of resisting US control on many occasions. In reality the Belgians, the Dutch, and the Italians could not afford AMX13s in the 1950s and their rearmament depended completely on US aid until after 1960. Thus early AMX13 sales were directed towards neutral nations. In 1951-1952 some of the first *preserie* vehicles were tested in Switzerland and in April 1952 Sweden received loan of a vehicle for potential adoption as the Swedish Army's battle tank. The AMX13 Mle 1958 was built exclusively for the export market and such customers bought large numbers of VTT Mle 56 and artillery variants. In 1964 the French became bold enough to propose license production of the AMX13 in the United States for friendly client states – perhaps recognizing that their armaments industry could not produce newer weapons like the AMX30 in volume at the same time as AMX13s for export.[38]

Europe:
Switzerland was the first export customer for the AMX13. In early 1950 the Swiss requirement for a replacement for the turretless G13 tank destroyer became urgent. The Swiss army required 500 modern tanks and embarked on a detailed evaluation of what was then available in Europe and the United States. An understanding was quickly reached with the French government to evaluate the AMX tank prototypes with the French army. A Swiss delegation visited Satory in 1951 and soon identified the AMX13 as a fast, powerfully armed weapon to counterattack airborne landings and protect infantry formations from enemy armour. The Mle 51s were purchased and there were separate negotiations to buy Centurions

which could not be filled until 1955 because of Britain's own requirements. One of the AMX13 prototypes was loaned to the Swiss for trials at high altitudes and under snowy conditions. The Mle 51 was adopted as the L Pzw 51 or *Leichter Panzerwagen 51* in December 1951 with an order for 200 vehicles. The first eight Swiss L Pz 51s (based on the Series 1 chassis) were delivered in 1952. The rush to fill the Swiss order delayed the re-equipment of French regiments but it raised the AMX13's international profile. The rest of the Swiss vehicles were based very closely on the French Series 2A chassis production batches and all were delivered by 1956. The L Pzw 51s were equipped for Swiss radios which were fitted at Thun.

The designation was changed to *Leichter Panzer 51 or L Pz 51* in 1954 and these vehicles were issued to four light tank regiments (*Leichter Panzer Abteilung 1*, *Leichter Panzer Abteilung 2*, *Leichter Panzer Abteilung 3*, and *Leichter Panzer Abteilung 4*). After 1961 the L Pz 51 served in 6 armoured reconnaissance battalions (*Aufklarungsbatalion 1, 3, 4, 6, 8* and *11*) until 1980. In 1958 four examples of the turreted 105mm *automoteur* were ordered, and deliveries to the Swiss artillery followed in 1960. This well-engineered field artillery vehicle was very similar in concept to the British Abbott 105mm SPG and tests were very successful. A single VCI was also purchased in 1959 to accompany the evaluation of the 105mm self-propelled gun, but the Swiss adopted the M113 as their standard tracked APC and the American M109 as their self-

A trio of newly delivered Swiss L Pz 51s during a live firing exercise. The presence of very early Mle 51 features such as the headlights without guards, the original sprocket design shared with the prototypes, and the exhaust muffler cover with 7 circular holes indicate that these were built to the Series 1 standard in 1952. The idler wheel is already the type seen on all Series 2A, 2B or 2C chassis, and may have been fitted after delivery. The Swiss tool racks mounted on the turret were very similar to the type used on the US M41. (*Stiftung Historisches Armeematerial Führungsunterstützung*)

country	year ordered	Mle 1951 (FL-10)	AMX13 F11	Mle 1958 (FL-12)	AMX13 C90	VTT/VCI Mle 56	Poseur de Pont Mle 57	Obusier OB 105 Mle 50 AU	Obusier 105 AU Casemate Tournant	Canon AM 155 F3 (AM 155mm Mk.F3)	CD Mle 55 ARV
Switzerland	1951	200 (1952-1958)	0	0	0	0	0	0	4	0	0
Venezuela	1954	36	0	0	36 (1988)	66 (1973-74)	4 (1973-74?)	0	0	12 (1978?)	4 (1973-74?)
Sweden	1954	1	0	0	0	0	0	0	0	0	0
Israel	1955	100	0	0	0	0	0	60	0	0	0
Peru	1956	30	0	78 (1968-69)	0	0	0	0	0	0	0
Egypt	1956	30	0	0	0	0	0	0	0	0	0
India	1956	164	0	0	0	0	0	0	0	0	0
Austria	1956-57, 1958	34+21 (1959)+17 (1960)	0	0	0	0	0	0	0	0	4 (1961)
Dominican Republic	1957	15	0	0	0	0	0	0	0	0	0
Indonesia	1960	175	0	0	0	32	10	4 (1963)	0	0	4 (1963)
Algeria	1962	44	At least 2, 1963?	0	0	0	0	0	0	0	0
Belgium	1962	0	0	0	0	554	0	0	0	0	0
Netherlands	1962	0	0	131	0	633		82 (1963-1964)	0	0	15 (1963)+13 (1964)
Cambodia	1963	20	0	0	0	0	0	0	0	0	0
Italy	1963	0	0	0	0	509	0	0	0	0	0
Cote d'Ivoire	1966	5	0	0	5 (1976)	0	0	0	0	0	0
Morocco	1977	120+ unknown number**	At least 4, 1960?	0	30	28	0	15 (1962)+ 30 (1967)	0	32 (1974)+ 32 (1981) + 10 (1996)	2
Argentina	1969	0	0	58	0	180*	2	0	0	8 (+ 4 in 1970)	0
Tunisia	1957 and 1970	15	0	0	15 (ex-French)	0	0	0	0	0	0

Country	Year											
Chile	1971	0	0	0	0	0	0	0	0	0	8 (1975) + 4 (1978)	0
Ecuador	1971	0	0	108 (1971-77)	0	93 (1976-79) + 12 mortar carriers	0	0	0	0	12 (1976-77)	0
Kuwait	1971	0	0	0	0	34	0	0	0	0	28	1
Lebanon	1972	42+ unknown number**	0	22	13	90	0	0	0	0	0	0
Guatemala	1974	8	0	0	0	0	0	0	0	0	0	0
Djibouti	1978	0	0	0	60	0	0	0	0	0	0	0
Qatar	1980	0	0	0	0	32	0	0	0	0	22	0
UAE	1980	0	0	0	0	11	0	0	0	0	20	0
Sudan	1981	0	0	0	0	5 artillery	0	0	0	0	6 or possibly 11	0
Cyprus	1989	0	0	0	0	12 (1989)	0	0	0	0	12 (probably 1989)	0
Singapore	1968, 1972, 1976	372**	0	0	0	0	0	0	0	0	0	0
Mexico	1994	0	0	0	0	409	0	0	0	0	0	0

*partial assembly in country

** supplied by 3rd party or aquired second hand

Note:
Netherlands converted some 26 VTTS into TOW-armed tank hunters.

A net-camouflaged L Pz 51 blocks a country road during an exercise in 1963. (*ETH-Bibliothek Zürich, Bildarchiv / Fotograf: Comet Photo AG (Zürich)/ Com_M12-0343-0002-0008 / CC BY-SA 4.0*)

Vehicle '232' on-the-march with the camouflage net lowered to improve hatch-out visibility for the commander and gunner. Note the commander's SIG-Stgw 57 assault rifle, which was slotted into the grab handle beside the commander's cupola. (*ETH-Bibliothek Zürich, Bildarchiv / Fotograf: Comet Photo AG (Zürich)/ Com_M12-0343-0002-0007 / CC BY-SA 4.0*)

The L Pz 51s preserved at Full and at Thun in Switzerland date from the first production batches and may be the oldest examples of the type still in existence. Their external appearance changed minimally despite having been updated incrementally through three normalisation programmes by Konstruktionswerkstätte (K+W) during their Swiss service. Other Swiss vehicles of similar vintage certainly made up a portion of the Mle 51s sold to Singapore and some of these subsequently underwent extensive modernization. (*Massimo Fotti*)

The L Pz 51 carried more spare track links than other AMX13 variants, and was normally fitted with steel track without rubber pads. (*Massimo Fotti*)

M-7807 has received a new driver's headlamp, one of the few alterations made by the Swiss Army to its L Pz 51s. (*Massimo Fotti*)

This L Pz 51 is still maintained in running condition, and splendidly shows the same configuration as when it served – which changed little between 1952 and the late 1970s. (*Massimo Fotti*)

propelled artillery system. The *Leichter Panzer 51* had a long and successful career in Swiss service but Swiss expectations of producing domestic tank designs in the 1960s precluded further tank purchases from France or Britain. The majority of the Swiss AMX13s were sold to Singapore following their retirement.[39]

The Swedes, unlike the Swiss, already produced tanks when they decided to buy a single foreign battle tank type to serve alongside upgraded Swedish wartime era tanks. Evaluation of one of the AMX13 prototypes took place between April 1952 and the following spring. Numerous issues with operation in snow and sub-zero temperatures were identified but the AMX13 impressed the Swedes. The British went on to win the Swedish order with the heavier Centurion but the notion of buying the FL10 as a potential turret for the Strv 74 persisted for some time. Sven Berge, one of the Swedish engineers evaluating the AMX13, was influenced by its design features. He saw the AMX13's automatic loader, trunnion mounted turret and 3-man crew as logical points to develop further; some of these persisted into the turretless S-Tank design a few years later.

It was DEFA's fondest ambition to sell AMX13 variants to West Germany, especially the VTT Mle 56. Between 1955 and 1960 numerous meetings between Joseph Molinié and German representatives took place. *Bundeswehr* officers paid extensive visits to the AMX facility at Satory and to the *Atelier de Roanne*, but West German intentions regarding the purchase of the AMX13 series were never comprehensively stated. French expectations of West German orders for AMX13 series vehicles lingered until 1960 but proved to be wishful thinking. The intention to co-produce a Franco-German medium tank added much confusion in French government circles, and bred a certain over-confidence in eventually securing West German orders. West Germany ordered trial quantities including five VTT Mle 56s in 1958, and then six OB 105 Mle 50 AUs, two more VTTs and a CD Mle 55 recovery vehicle in 1959. The Germans did buy French armoured vehicles; in 1956 they ordered 2,000 Hotchkiss carriers but hopes that the VTT Mle 56 would be selected as the *Bundeswehr*'s standard APC had evaporated by 1960.[40]

The AMX13 Mle 51 was procured for the Austrian *Bundesheer* in response to the Hungarian uprising in 1956 and its good performance in Alpine regions. Both 2C and 2D type chassis figured in the seventy-two tank order along with three Mle 55 recovery vehicles. They entered service in 1957 at the *Panzertruppenschule* at Götzendorf alongside T34-85s, M24s and M47s. Along with British Charioteers the AMX13 Mle 51 was employed by the Austrians as a tank hunter. In 1964 the Mle 51s were concentrated in *Jaeger Brigade 7*'s *Panzerjaegerkompanie 7* as the brigade antitank defence. *Panzer Abteilung 1* at Weiner Neustadt was formed with the remainder of the AMX13s at the *Panzerjägerschulabteilung*. The AMX13 Mle 51 was replaced in Austrian service in 1967-68 as the armoured corps standardized on the M60. The surplus Austrian AMX13s seemed for a time destined for sale to Yugoslavia, or subsequently back to SOFMA during 1970; they were eventually scrapped between 1971 and 1977. Although the FL12 turret was selected to arm the Saurer SK105 chosen to replace the Mle 51 in Austrian service, none were issued to the *Bundesheer* until 1972.[41]

French efforts to sell the other FINABEL members the AMX13 series were more fruitful than the efforts to sell it in West Germany. The Netherlands, Belgium and Italy all bought significant numbers. The Italian vehicles, which were all VTT Mle 56 derived VCI armoured personnel carriers, were paid for by US offshore credits. In Belgium the *Constructions*

An AMX13 Mle 51 with the Type 2D chassis is preserved (together with a Mle 55 recovery vehicle in the right background) at the Austrian *Heeresgeschichtliches Museum* (HGM) in Vienna. (*Jérôme Hadacek Collection*)

The pair of black-coloured IR driving lights and the two sets of triple 80mm smoke grenade launchers on the HGM's Mle 51 exhibit were probably fitted in the later years as these were not seen on the vehicles according to archival photos of the early 1960s from the Austrian National Library. (*Jérôme Hadacek Collection*)

Like its companion Mle 51, the Mle 55 recovery vehicle at the HGM had also been retrofitted with IR driving lights and 80mm smoke grenade launchers. The Mle 55s of the Austrian Army belonged to the later production batch as evident by the presence of four support rollers which are features of the Type 2D chassis. Note also the two large patches of anti-slip coating applied to the front upper slope of the hull. (*Jérôme Hadacek Collection*)

To improve the survivability of the Mle 55 recovery vehicles, the Austrians installed a total of four banks of triple 80mm smoke grenade launchers of which two were mounted within a guard frame at the mid-front edge of the superstructure. Note that this HGM exhibit is missing the 80mm launcher tubes. (*Jérôme Hadacek Collection*)

Rear left view of the HRM Mle 55 recovery vehicle. The empty frames for the two rear banks of smoke grenade launchers can be seen at both ends of the stowed tow bars above the stabilizing spades. Note the later style rubber-padded tracks. (*Jérôme Hadacek Collection*)

Ferroviaires du Centre (CFC) firm in Familleureux, Hainaut, was licensed to build 523 of the 550 Mle 56 VCIs ordered for the Belgian army. The CFC plant produced 92 VCIs in 1962, 243 in 1963 and 186 in 1964 before the order was completed. Argentina eventually produced a significant portion of their VCI order after 1968 by similar means. The Belgian production vehicles included 305 Mle 56 VTT standard armoured personnel carriers armed with the 38 CALF 7.62mm turret which served in six mechanized infantry regiments. The order also included seventy-two command post versions, ninety 81mm mortar carrier versions, and fifty-eight cargo versions. A smaller batch for thirty VTT Mle 56s fitted out as ENTAC missile launcher vehicles served as tank destroyers. The VTT Mle 56 had a long and relatively uneventful career in the Belgian Army, and all were replaced by 1988 with British CVRT and American M113 based vehicles.[42]

In March 1961 the *Koninklijke Landmacht* (Royal Netherlands Army) placed the largest European order for 727 AMX13 series vehicles to replace their M24 light tanks and the US halftracks. The order rose later to 846 vehicles. These included 131 Mle 58 light tanks, 34 CD Mle 55 recovery vehicles (known as PRB for *Pantser Rups Berging*), and 82 self-propelled guns based on a modernised version of the OB 105 Mle 50 AU adopted in 1963 as the PRA (full

Rear oblique view of a Belgian VTT Mle 56 on parade. A pair of stowage baskets has been fitted onto the lower part of the rear doors. (*Arthur Chapman*)

designation *105mm, Houwitzer, AMX Pantser Rups Artillerie L30*) to replace older pieces like the 25 pounder. The rest of the order was made up of VTT Mle 56s, which were known as the PRI (*Pantser, Rups, Infanterie*) in Dutch service.

The Netherlands were the first customer to order the AMX13 Mle 58. Extensive trials took place in late 1960 at the Le Courtine camp then already leased from the French army to train Centurion crews. After delivery, a significant list of defects appeared. In late 1963 DEFA engineers under Joseph Molinié evaluated and corrected 24 problems identified by the Netherlands army before the units equipped with AMX13 series vehicles could be considered fit for active duty. Deliveries from France continued and while many defects were of a minor nature with the Mle 56 VTT, the most worrying problem was defective fittings, armour plate and castings in some of the FL12 turrets which were repaired or replaced. The culprit was the greater recoil of the CN-105-57, which caused stress cracks. The problems associated with the Dutch orders brought a number of improvements to the FL12 turret and the 105mm gun's muzzle brake. By May 1965, the scandal had passed and the Mle 58 light tank sold well thereafter as an export, although the quality problems of 1963 may have been significant in the failure of French efforts to sell the AMX30 to the Netherlands in the same period.[43]

The Mle 58 was designated *Lichte Tank: met Kanon 105 mm, L 44, type 2D (AMX)* in KL service and was used by the cavalry in the KL's divisional reconnaissance units *(verkenningsbataljons)* for the 1st and 4th Mechanized Divisions in the 1960s. The 102nd and 103rd reconnaissance battalions and the 11th, 12th, 13th, 41st, 42nd and 43rd independent reconnaissance squadrons

An Mle 58 in service with the Royal Netherlands Army (*Koninklijke Landmacht*, abbreviated to KL) in 1979 at Vlieland, an important training centre where Centurion, Leopard 1 and AMX13 crews were trained in gunnery in annual camps. (*Arend Jan Faber*)

The Mle 58 experienced some well publicized teething problems when it was first introduced but it went on to serve the KL successfully for nearly 20 years. The KL's Mle 58s featured a large searchlight mounted on the right side of the turret. The FN MAG 58 was mounted as the standard coaxial weapon and on the commander's station for local defence. (*Arend Jan Faber*)

A Royal Netherlands Army AMX13 seen in 1979. The Mle 58 featured infrared lamps as standard and the front splash board conceals the larger gun crutch required by the 105mm gun. (*Arend Jan Faber*)

The driver's foul weather hood employed on the KL's Mle 58s. This simple device was intended to keep the driver dry in wet weather. (*Arend Jan Faber*)

The instrument panel and controls at the driver's station on a Dutch Mle 58. These were similar in all versions of the AMX13 – with, of course, the exception of labelling. (*Arend Jan Faber*)

Now preserved in the Netherlands, this former KL operated Mle 58 is seen from above, showing the standard Dutch modifications. The MAG58 GPMG is fitted to the commander's cupola, the bracket plate for the infrared searchlight on the right side of the turret and the Dutch wireless aerials are seen secured for road movement. (*Jakko Westerbekke*)

were all part of the larger *Regiment Huzaren van Boreels*. A *verkenningsbataljon* was made up of three squadrons *(verkenningseskadrons)* each of which included three reconnaissance platoons. The reconnaissance platoon included a command group, two Mle 58s, a scout group in PRIs and a support group. The Mle 58 also served as a tank hunter manned by the artillery arm in the KL's infantry brigades from 1962 until the early 1980s. A total of six independent antitank artillery batteries employed the Mle 58 between 1963

Decal from the *Vlieland Cavalerie Schiet* Kamp gunnery establishment from the late 1970s. Dutch Mle 58 crews were tested annually at the Vlieland ranges, alongside counterparts in Centurions and Leopard 1s. (*Arend Jan Faber Collection*)

A *Pantser Rups Infanterie* of the *Limburgse Jagers* in 1972. It is equipped with a forward firing 3-barrel smoke discharger on the right side of the engine deck and with the S470 cupola, although the 12.7 mm MG is not fitted. The KL also operated a small number of PRIs fitted with the CAFL 38 turret. (*Jan Barnier*)

and 1975, each incorporating fifteen vehicles in three platoons of five tanks. These were numbered the 11th, 13th, 42nd, 12th (reserve), 52nd and 53rd Antitank Batteries (Atbt abbreviated from *Antitankbatterij*). The KL's reconnaissance units retired their last Mle 58s in 1983 as Leopard 1s became available following the adoption of the Leopard 2.[44]

The new mechanised infantry arm ordered a total of 345 PRIs (full designation *Gevechtsvoertuig, Pantser, Rups, Infanterie: Type 2D*), mainly armed with the S470 12.7mm machine-gun cupola. The AMX-PRI included several sub-types equipped for different roles. Of the 345 PRIs, 162 were command post vehicles (known as PR *Commando* or PRCO), forty-six PRIs were configured as cargo transports (PRVR or PR *Vracht*), and forty-six were fitted as PRGWT (or ambulance *Gewondentransport*). These broadly conformed to the French VTT Mle 56 variants. Sixty-seven of the remainder were converted in the Netherlands into 81mm mortar carriers PRMR (or PR *Mortiertrekker*), and twenty-six into TOW missile armed tank hunters. Prior to the TOW missile's adoption in the KL, the 106mm recoiless rifle was employed on the PRI to provide an antitank vehicle for the infantry. The TOW launch vehicles were designated PR *Antitank met TOW*, or PRAT. The S470 cupola was modified to mount the TOW launcher. The AMX PRI was used in the *41e Pantser Infanterie Bataljon Stoottroepen*, the *47e Pantser Infanterie Bataljon Menno Coehoorn*, *16e* and *42e Pantser Infanterie Bataljon Limburgse Jagers*, the *17e Pantser Infanterie Bataljon Chassé* and in the *14e Pantser Infanterie Bataljon*. The *103e Verkeningeskadron* (the *Huzaren van Boreels*) also used the AMX PRI. The KL was never

The Cypriot National Guard operates a complete AM F3 regiment, acquired in 1989 with the AMX30B2 from France. The vehicles seen here were photographed in 2015. (*Proelasi/Duke*)

satisfied with the rate of availability of the PRI and, in 1978, it was replaced in service with the YPR-765.[45]

The AMX PRA 105mm self-propelled gun served in regiments of the KL's Field and Horse Artillery for 20 years. In 1963, the first guns entered service in the 12th, 41st and 43rd *Afdeling Veldartillerie*. A fourth (horse) artillery regiment, the *11e Afdeling Rijdende Artillerie* was equipped in 1969. The 42[e], 13[e] (Reserve) and 51e (Reserve) *Afdeling Veldartillerie* regiments all received the PRA in 1970. The PRA regiments employed a 3 battery structure (6 guns per battery) with 18 guns per regiment. After 1982 the PRA was replaced in KL service by the more heavily armed M109 155mm self-propelled gun.[46]

Africa, The Middle East and Asia:

India was the second foreign customer to adopt the Mle 51 in 1954, ordering 150 Mle 51s with deliveries starting the following year. Indian enthusiasm for the AMX13 was such that local production of the Mle 51 and its 75mm ammunition was investigated in depth by the Indians in 1963-1964 with SOFMA. DEFA and DGA engineers visited India and blueprints were transferred to the Indian authorities. The production licence was never granted and the matter was dropped in the mid-1960s after India obtained a licence to produce the Vickers Medium Tank. The Indian AMX13s were used in combat successfully in 1962 and 1965 and were later sold on to Singapore in the 1970s.[47]

An Israeli military attaché was present at the Aberdeen Proving Ground trials of the AMX13 in 1952. The United States and Great Britain were then both unwilling to sell Israel arms; France followed a similar line while pressing its opportunities to sell arms elsewhere in the Middle East. In February 1956 SOFMA were negotiating the sale of fifty Mle 51s, and 20 OB 105 Mle 50 AUs to Syria, a country with strong ties to France. In the same period thirty Mle 51s and some Shermans fitted with FL10 turrets were sold to Egypt. Franco-Egyptian attitudes hardened after July 1956 and France cancelled arms sales to Nasser's government. The Syrian arms deal also was never concluded. An Israeli order for sixty Mle 51s was negotiated, however, and followed by orders for forty more (and for 20 OB 105 Mle 50 AUs). The Israeli order also included CN 75-50 guns suitable for rearming the *Tsahal*'s Sherman fleet and other French arms worth over $80 million. The new Mle 51s were blooded shortly after delivery in the 1956 Arab Israeli War (or Suez Crisis).[48]

Morocco was an early customer for the AMX13, purchasing seventeen Mle 51s in 1956 followed by a second order in 1965 for twenty-eight vehicles. The Mle 51 saw action against Polisario guerillas in the mid-1970s during the Western Sahara War, and it is believed that at least four vehicles were captured. Israel is believed to have sold Morocco a number of her own surplus Mle 51s to replace Moroccan losses. France also sold Morocco fifteen OB 105 Mle 50 AUs in 1963, probably built to a similar standard to the Netherlands and Indonesian vehicles ordered at the same time. Another thirty were ordered in 1968. In 1974 and 1981 Morocco bought two thirty-two gun batches of the more powerful AM F3, possibly with Saudi financial assistance, along with two CD Mle 55 recovery vehicles and twenty Mle 56 VCIs configured as artillery support versions (some which were equipped with RATAC radar). In 1991 France sold a final 10-gun AM F3 batch to Morocco, although these may have been refurbished vehicles from their own surplus artillery stocks. Tunisia also purchased two lots of AMX13s, fifteen Mle 51s in 1957 and fifteen newly converted AMX13 C90s in 1968. These were eventually replaced

The AMX13 Mle 51 served in two regiments (8th Cavalry and 20th Lancer) of the Indian Army till the early 1970s. It was subsequently employed by three independent reconnaissance squadrons (90th Recce Sqn of the Poona Horse, 92nd Recce Sqn of the 18 Cavalry and 93rd Recce Sqn of the 65th Armoured Regiment). (*Mohit S, used under CC BY 2.0*)

This AMX13 Mle 51 with Type 2C chassis is preserved in the Cavalry Tank Museum at Ahmednagar, India. Note the "Golden Axe" emblem of the 12th Infantry Division on the left fender and the unique antenna mountings of the Indian Mle 51s. (*Mohit S, used under CC BY 2.0*)

By the 1970s, the Indian Mle 51s became increasingly ineffective on the battlefield with the appearance of the Pakistani T-59 MBTs, which is a Chinese version of the Russian T-54. A good number of the Indian Mle 51 stock was subsequently sold and transferred to Singapore between 1973 and 1975. (*Mohit S, used under CC BY 2.0*)

The M4/FL10 hybrid was developed in France and adopted by the Egyptians. These were Shermans with their regular turret replaced by the FL10 turrets of the AMX13 Mle 51. A number of these conversions were performed by Batignolles-Chatillon and delivered to Egypt around 1955. (*Peter Lau*)

The M4/FL10 participated in both the 1956 and 1967 wars. This example at the Yad La-Shiryon at Latrun, Israel was captured by the IDF near Al Arish during the Six Day War. (*Peter Lau*)

with Austrian SK105s and none remain in service. Algeria inherited forty-four ex-French army AMX13s (including several AMX13 FL11s) in 1962 as French forces were drawn down, and these became the core of the Armée Nationale Populaire's armoured force. Soviet supplied vehicles replaced the Algerian AMX13s in the 1980s and no further variants were acquired.

Lebanon was an important user of the AMX13 in the Middle East, purchasing forty-two Mle 51s in 1972 along with twenty-two Mle 58s. At least ninety Mle 56 VCIs were also purchased directly from France that year. A smaller purchase of used AMX13 C90s followed in the late 1970s. In 1987 the Lebanese Army was believed to have sixty operational AMX13 Mle 51s, Mle 58s and C90s and about eighty Mle 56 VCIs, although estimates have ranged at various times from forty to over one hundred light tanks. It is possible that some of the Lebanese vehicles were supplied by Israel to make up losses suffered in the country's civil wars. The number of AMX13s serving in the government's army, in breakaway army elements and in militias has varied throughout the 1980s and since. Today none of the Lebanese AMX13 lights tanks or Mle 56 VCIs is believed to remain operational.[49]

Kuwait was one of the very first countries to order the AM F3 in 1967 with an order for ten vehicles, with repeat orders for eight and ten vehicles in 1974 and 1982. Creusot-Loire

Newly delivered AMX13 Mle 51 tanks parading through Ben Yehuda Street in Tel Aviv on the Independence Day in 1955. These vehicles are some of the earliest delivered to Israel, with the Series 2A chassis. In the 1956 Suez Crisis the Mle 51 was Israel's most modern battle tank. (*Cohen Fritz / Israel Government Press Office*)

Mle 51s undergoing maintenance in an army workshop in October 1955. Note the early Type 2A chassis with its sloped tool bins. (*Israeli Government Press Office*)

Following the Sinai campaign, a Swedish officer from the UNEF talks with members of an Israeli Mle 51 crew before the Israeli withdrawal from Rafah in early 1957. The gunner and driver of this tank are seen to be wearing the Russian style padded helmet whereas the tank commander has donned the traditional armour black beret. (*Israeli Government Press Office*)

A column of Israeli Mle 51s headed for the Israeli border during the UN-supervised withdrawal from Rafah. (*Israeli Government Press Office*)

IDF Mle 51 tanks parading at the University Stadium on Independence Day 1958. The tanks in the picture, featuring the FL10A turret on a Type B chassis, may have been delivered after the 1956 war. (*Israel Government Press Office*)

The IDF modified some of their Mle 51s with sand skirts and a slightly raised turret platform sometime around 1957. The picture shows such a vehicle on a Type 2B chassis. (*Claude Dubary*)

An IDF Mle 51 alongside an M50 Isherman in 1963. Both of these tanks mounted the CN-75-50 75mm gun. (*Cohen Fritz/ Israeli Government Press Office*)

An IDF Mle 51 with the Type 2C hull (identifiable by the triangular head protector) photographed during manoeuvres in the Negev desert in 1965. Note that the crews of this vehicle wore what appears to be the WW2 US M38 tanker helmet. (*Milner Moshe/ Israeli Government Press Office*)

Two abandoned Lebanese Mle 56 VCIs were captured by the IDF during the 1982 Operation Peace for Galilee; one is on display at the Yad La-Shiryon. This vehicle belongs to the later production batches as it is equipped with the S 470 cupola armed with a 12.7mm heavy machine gun. (*Peter Lau*)

successfully marketed the Mle 56 VCI (in several configurations), and the AM F3 quite successfully in the Arabian Peninsula for some time after the AMX13 Mle 51 and Mle 58s had ceased to attract orders (by the mid-1970s France was far more interested in selling potential clients the AMX30B). Kuwait purchased thirty-four Mle 56 VCIs in 1982 to support its artillery batteries. The United Arab Emirates purchased eleven Mle 56 VCIs in 1975 followed by twenty AM F3s in 1978. Qatar ordered thirty-three Mle 56 VCIs in 1979 to support twenty-two AM F3s in 1979. Both countries, unlike the Kuwaitis, adopted the AMX30B main battle tank in the same period. Sudan purchased five artillery-support Mle 56 VCIs and six AM F3s in 1981, although the number of self-propelled pieces may have in fact amounted to eleven vehicles. The Cypriot National Guard was one of the last countries to buy the AM F3, their purchase of twelve vehicles coinciding with their adoption of the AMX30B2 in 1989.[50]

The first AMX13s were procured for the Indonesian army (TNI-AD) between 1960 and 1965 as part of the arms buildup required for President Sukarno's Trikora campaign to annex West Irian (Western Papua) from the Dutch. A total of fifty-seven Mle 51 light tanks, twenty-two Mle 56 VCIs, two Mle 55 recovery vehicles, four PP F1 bridge layers and four OB 105 Mle 50 AU self-propelled gun were supplied to the TNI-AD by France, who were selling the Netherlands the AMX13 in the same period. This piece of post-colonial duplicity could not have sat well with France's NATO ally but it was not unique in the period. The tanks served as the main equipment in the TNI-AD's Armoured Cavalry Tank battalions (referred to as "*yonkavs*" from *Battalyon Kavalrie*, the standard tank-equipped unit) and some may remain in service to this day.[51]

An Indonesian AMX13 Mle 51 (Type 2D chassis) disembarking from a LST (Landing Ship Tank) of the Indonesian Navy. Sealifting operations are essential as Indonesia is the world largest archipelago with over 17,000 islands. (*Vicky Gosal*)

A TNI-AD Mle 51 that is camouflaged with natural foliage to break its shape and cover the tell-tale shadow underneath the chassis. When done skillfully the crew will gain the critical element of surprise over their opponent. (*Vicky Gosal*)

The TNI-AD operates a mixture of both the 75mm-armed Mle 51 and the 105mm-armed Mle 58 tanks. The Mle 51s seen here were acquired from France during the early 1960s. (*Vicky Gosal*)

South America:

South America has felt the weight of American interest and influence throughout the 20th Century, and French arms sales in the region have often met with American displeasure. The area has been subject to local arms races between neighbouring regimes and has many long standing territorial disputes. The rough terrain and steep hill country in many South American nations made the light AMX13 an ideal weapon. National armies employed the AMX13 as a conventional light tank and their AMX13 fleets were carefully husbanded for decades. Today five South American countries still operate vehicles from the AMX13 family.[52]

Venezuela was the first South American country to buy the AMX 13 Mle 1951. In April 1953 a Mle 51 light tank arrived from France for evaluation by the Venezuelan army. The evaluation led to an order for thirty-six Mle 51 light tanks on 10 February 1954. They arrived in 1955 and were used to form the *Bravos de Apure* armoured battalion based at San Juan de los Morros. Peru followed in 1956 with an order for thirty Mle 51s. A second Peruvian order for seventy-eight of the more powrfully armed Mle 58 followed in 1968. In the early 1970s the Venezuelan army purchased eighteen AM F3 self-propelled 155mm howitzers and fifty VTT Mle 56s of different versions from Creusot-Loire. The Venezuelan VTT Mle 65 order included the troop carrier version (VTT-VCI), and smaller numbers of command vehicles (VTT-PC), 81mm mortar carriers (VTT-PM), armoured ambulances (VTT-TB,) and artillery fire control vehicles (VTT-LT) to accompany the AM F3s.

When the American government refused the Dominican Republic's requests for military equipment in the 1950s, President Rafael Trujillo turned to SOFMA. The Dominican government ordered fifteen Mle 51s from France and received them in October 1959. Upon arrival, the new tanks were transferred to the armoured battalion of the Dominican Military Aviation Corps (AMD) and the vehicles were assigned numbers from 501 to 515. Following Trujillo's assassination in 1961 the tanks were transferred to the Armed Forces Training Centre (CEFA *Centro de Enseñanza de las Fuerzas Armadas*) at the San Isidro Air Base.

Argentina's army adopted the AMX13 because of American refusals to sell modern weapons. The Argentinian *Ejercito* turned to European arms manufacturers. The army urgently needed 120 tanks, 180 APCs for the infantry, and twenty-four 155mm self-propelled guns and support vehicles. An important caveat in the Argentinian requirement was to obtain a licence to undertake local AFV production to achieve a measure of self-sufficiency in the country's defence needs. Consideration was given to buying the AMX30B or the AMX13 Mle 58 from France, and an order was placed with SOFMA for fifty-eight Mle 58s in 1967. In February 1968 Argentinian officials awarded a contract to SOFMA to establish a production line in Argentina for the local assembly of the VTT Mle 56.[53]

Plans were also made to produce an indigenous medium tank. The Mle 58 did not entirely meet the expectations of the Argentinians due partly to its small size and also its thin armour. It served in cavalry reconnaissance regiments, most recently in the *Regimiento de Caballería de Exploración 5* at Salta and the *Regimiento de Caballería de Exploración 15* in Campo de los Andes close to the Chilean border. The continued requirement for a 15-tonne light tank for use in

The VTT SAN continues to serve in the armoured ambulance role in the *Ejército Nacional de la República Bolivariana de Venezuela*. The vehicle seen here was participating in a parade alongside AMX30V MBTs and carries field stretchers on each side of the hull. (*Collection Danter César*)

The VTT SAN incorporated the Mle 51 commander's cupola instead of the CAFL 38 turret or the S470 cupola. The VTT's chassis was based on a slightly lengthened Type 2D chassis and was manufactured alongside the Mle 51 Type 2D and Mle 58 light tanks. (*Collection Danter César*)

As in most armies, Venezuelan ambulance vehicles carry large Red Cross markings. Note this vehicle carries two red basket stretchers instead of field stretchers. (*Danter César Cappelini Mota*)

The VTT SAN has seen very little modification during its long career in Venezuelan service. The crew of this VTT SAN is taking a quick rest break on top of their vehicle. (*Carlos Antonio Arroyo Alonso*)

The Venezuelan VTT SAN has carried an overall semi-gloss *vert armée* livery as well as the two tone disruptive camouflage seen here. The national insignia is carried on the front and sides. (*Carlos Antonio Arroyo Alonso*)

The armoured 81mm mortar carrier version of the VTT Mle 56 was never purchased by the French Army, but was marketed by Creusot-Loire and saw service in other countries in several configurations. This Venezuelan example has all its hatches in the open position. (*Carlos Antonio Arroyo Alonso*)

Equipped with the CAFL 38 turret, this VTT Mle 56 is employed as a command vehicle in Venezuelan service. (*Collection Claude Dubary*)

A Venezuelan army command vehicle. The VTT Mle 56 was protected from artillery splinters and small arms, and the crew's ability to fight from the vehicle made it one of the mo most advanced armoured personnel carriers of its time. (*Collection Danter César*)

The Venezuelan Army will probably retain some AMX13 variants in service for years to come. (*Collection Danter César*)

One of the original Mle 51s on display in Venezuela. Venezuela placed most of its Mle 51s into storage, but, while spare or reconditioned parts remain available, there is always the possibility that these will be upgraded in the future. (*Collection Danter César*)

The AM 155 F3 remains in regular service in the *Ejército Nacional de la República Bolivariana de Venezuela*. (*Collection Danter César*)

The Peruvian Mle 58 tanks were delivered between 1968 and 1969. Note the Israeli style black plastic jerry can on the side of the turret. (*US Government Photo via Steven Zaloga*)

Dominican AMX13 Mle 51s (type 2D Chassis) and a Landsverk L-60 light tank assemble prior to a parade. The "E.N." under the vehicle number of the leading Mle 51 stands for *Ejército Nacional* which is National Army in Spanish. The pintle-mounted 0.3 Calibre Browning machine gun on the Mle 51s was introduced after the 1965 civil war. (*US Government Photo via Steven Zaloga*)

areas with limited infrastructure, where heavier vehicles could not operate, were met when the Mle 58s were supplemented by orders for 118 Austrian SK105 Kuirassiers. The SK105 also employed the FL12 turret and used the same ammunition. The Mle 58s were kept in service and were modified with new Deutz diesel engines and MAG58 coaxial weapons in 1979 (and underwent a second rebuild programme in 1999).

The licensed production (or more appropriately local assembly) of 180 VTT Mle 56s marked Argentina's re-entry into AFV manufacture, and this was eventually followed by licenced production of the Thyssen-Henschel designed *Tanque Argentino Mediano*. The AMX13 and SK105 were both projected for replacement in the Argentinian army by the light *Patagón* tank announced in 2003. The *Patagón* was a rebuilt SK105 hull re-turreted with the rebuilt and modernized FL12 turrets of decommissioned Mle 58s. The main advantage of the *Patagón* over the SK105 is believed to be the ability to fire the 105mm APFSDS-T round. The redundant Mle 58 hulls would have been used to supply spare parts for the Argentinian AM F3 and VTT Mle 56. A prototype and four conversions were completed under Steyr supervision before being cancelled in 2008 due to cost concerns. Only forty-one Mle 58s and thirty-one VTTs remained in service by 2010 in the two cavalry regiments and in the infantry. By the time of the Mle 58's

Argentina purchased the AMX13 Mle 58 in the late 1960s and licence-produced the VTT Mle 56. Argentina had already produced the DL43 Nahuel medium tank in the 1940s, but economic factors and the availability of cheap surplus AFVs in the postwar period doomed national aspirations of tank production until the late 1970s. Argentina helped train the Ecuadorean Army's first AMX13 crews in Argentina, seen here in 1973. (*General Jorge Andrade Piedra*)

As delivered the Argentinian Mle 58s were equipped with the MAC31 co-axial machinegun and with tracks lacking the rubber pads (although the latter were introduced later). The MAG58 General Purpose Machinegun was quickly fitted by the Argentinian Army on the commander's cupola. These vehicles were photographed moving at high speed during driver training for Ecuadorean crews in 1973. (*General Jorge Andrade Piedra*)

The Argentinian *Ejército* employed the Mle 58 for many years, latterly in the defence of the southern and western border areas against Chilean incursions. This preserved example is painted in overall olive drab. The Mle 58s were most likely delivered in *vert armée* and were built at the Le Creusot plant. (*Eugenio Diaz*)

The Deutz diesel engine retrofitting work for the Argentinian Mle 58s was performed by the local engineering company, TENSA (Talleres Electrometalúrgicos Norte S.A.). For the integration of the new engine, the top deck of the engine compartment was rebuilt with a large rectangular grille with diagonal slates; a new box was also constructed upon the right track fender to house the engine's ancillary equipment. (*Walter Scavuzzo*)

Frontal view of a modernized Mle 58 which is preserved at the *Museo Histórico del Ejercito Argentino*. Note the asymmetric profile of the vehicle after the addition of the engine ancillary equipment box on the right track fender. (*Walter Scavuzzo*)

retirement in 2012, only twenty-six were still operable. All twenty-four AM F3s are still believed to remain in service with the Argentinian artillery.[54]

Ecuador acquired the largest South American AMX13 fleet with an order of 108 Mle 58s delivered in the early 1970s in response to the modernization of Peru's armoured force. The order was followed by orders for other vehicles from the AMX13 family in order to rationalize logistics across all combat arms. Ecuadorean personnel trained in Argentina in 1973 to familiarize the crews with their new vehicles which replaced early M3 Light Tank variants in service. The new Mle 58s were concentrated in the 3rd *Azuay* Reconnaissance Group in

Quito, but moved to Riobamba to form the 1st *Galapagos* Armoured Brigade in March 1974. The brigade's strength was heavily dependent on AMX13 series AFVs, fielding AMX13 Mle 58s in the 1st *Machala* Tank Group, VTT Mle 56s in the 1st *Riobamba* Armored Infantry Battalion and the AM F3's in the 11th *Teniente Rodriguez* Self-Propelled Artillery Group.

When the orders were complete in 1977, and the Ecuadorian AMX13 fleet also included the M55 recovery vehicle and four versions of the VTT Mle 56. In October 1977, the 2nd *Azuay* Tank Group was raised using a portion of the vehicles from the 1st *Machala* Tank Group and vehicles from the School of Amoured Forces. In 1987, the army merged the armoured and cavalry branches and the armoured brigade was re-designated the 11th *Galapagos* Cavalry Brigade. As part of this reformation, the number of organic tanks in a tank group was reduced from fifty-four to thirty-one. During the 1981 and 1995 Ecuadorian-Peruvian border conflicts, the *Galapagos* brigade deployed to the province of El Oro to repulse an expected attack from Peru but was not engaged.[55]

Chile was an early customer of the heavier AMX30B in the 1970s but the Pinochet coup resulted in socialist pressure within France to block arms sales to the new government. Chile negotiated the completion of the purchase of twelve AM F3s in 1979 after protracted refusals by the French government and all were delivered by 1981. The guns are known as *Autopropulsado ATP 155mm F3* and alternately as *AMX13 Mk F3 de 155 mm* in Chilean service. These were deployed in two 6-gun artillery groups in the North and South of the country for

Like many South American Armies, the Ecuadorean armoured force was based on obsolete vehicles such as the M3A1 Light Tank until the AMX13 arrived. The Ecuadorean army's Mle 58s were purchased along with the VTT Mle 56, CN 155 AM F3 and M113 in the early 1970s, allowing its cavalry, infantry and artillery arms to operate with modern equipment in an integrated mechanized formation- the Galapagos Brigade. (*General Jorge Andrade Piedra*)

The Ecuadorean armoured cavalry brigade's first AMX13 crewmen received training in Argentina in the early 1970s. This is an Ecuadorean Mle 58 seen shortly after delivery in the early 1970s. Like in all of the South American armies, equipment in the Ecuadorean *Ejército* was carefully maintained through long service lives spanning several decades, and this vehicle could still be in service. The Ecuadorean Galapagos Armoured Cavalry Brigade evolved as a balanced force including reconnaissance troops, light tanks, mechanized infantry and self-propelled artillery. One of its principal roles was to deter Peruvian cross-border incursions. (*General Jorge Andrade Piedra*)

The Mle 58's CN-105-57 was one of the most powerful tank guns fielded on the South American continent. The Ecuadorean crews seen here are preparing to load 105mm ammunition from standard French wooden packing cases. They are wearing a mixture of US and locally manufactured uniforms. (*General Jorge Andrade Piedra*)

A column of Mle 58s, probably from the 1st Machala tank group. The tarps covering these vehicles are being removed prior to an inspection. (*Jorge Andrade Piedra*)

25 years. Since 2007 these guns have served in *Grupo de Artillería N° 7 Wood*, the artillery detachment of the *4ª Brigada Acorazada* (4th Armoured Brigade) *Chorrillos*, stationed in the South. The ATP 155mm F3 were supplemented in 2009 by refurbished M109 series guns bought from the United States and may now be replaced.[56]

Second Hand Users:

In the early 1970s Creusot-Loire rationalized the AMX13 family while AM F3 orders for the French artillery were completed. In the meantime the Mle 58 was successfully marketed in South America and the AM 155mm F3 was ordered by customers on several continents. Creusot-Loire received few orders from the French army after the French AM F3 orders were completed and the company faced increasing challenges to its survival in the 1980s. The market for used AMX13s continued to grow as many Mle 51s, Mle 58s and VTTs were retired and rebuilt for second-hand customers. The Netherlands replaced the AMX13 family in the early 1980s selling surplus vehicles to Indonesia. The Indonesian-Dutch AMX acquisition program known as Project Beta lasted from 1976 until 1983. It began with the transfer of nearly 600 PRI armoured personnel carriers and later included about 130 Mle 58 light tanks, over 30 Mle 55 recovery vehicles and around 80 PRA 105mm SPGs. The ex-PRI armoured personnel carriers included command post and mortar carrier versions. All of the former KL vehicles were overhauled by RDM & Wilton Fijennoord of the Netherlands before delivery to Indonesia where they were employed in armoured cavalry to replace the strategic reserve's older Mle 51 light tanks and to equip the territorial cavalry battalions; they were also used in the armoured infantry and to increase the number of armoured artillery regiments.[57]

After Singapore's independence in 1965 its government sought Israeli expertise to develop its armed forces (which then consisted of two nominal infantry battalions). In 1967 the Singapore ministry of defence (MID) decided to create an armoured unit equipped with tanks and armoured cars. The IDF advisors recommended the Mle 51 after studying the likely area of operations and lessons from local wartime Japanese operations. The light and compact AMX13 was ideal for the task and could cross the bridges then available in the area. In January 1968, a deal for the supply of seventy-two ex-IDF AMX13s was negotiated. Both parties benefitted; Israel was able to sell surplus vehicles and Singapore could use the AMX13 to make a quantum leap forward in her defence capability. Once deployed the AMX13s were the only tank force in the Malaya Peninsula for many years.[58]

The Singapore Defence Force sent thirty-six officers to Israel on 31 December 1968 to train with the IDF for 4 months to learn the technical and operational aspects of the AMX13. These officers formed the nucleus of the 40th Singapore Armoured Battalion (40 SAB, Singapore's first armoured unit) in September 1969. In June 1969, the first thirty refurbished

The Mle 58 tanks of the TNI-AD such as the one depicted here were procured from the Netherlands. These vehicles retained most of the original Dutch features including the searchlight mounting bracket, smoke grenade launchers and the commander's machine-gun mount. (*TNI-AD / Yonkav 3*)

The Mle 56 VTTs of the Indonesian Army originated from both the French and Dutch stocks with the oldest vehicles having served since the early 1960s. (*TNI-AD/Yonkav 3*)

AMX13s had arrived and forty-two more followed that September. As the armoured force expanded 150 more AMX13s were obtained from India in the early 1970s and 150 were bought from Switzerland later in the decade. In May 1978, the Singapore Automotive Engineering (SAE) company was tasked to perform a Limited Depot Overhaul (LDO) programme to restore the tanks to near original condition. The refurbishment work began in February 1979. The tanks were stripped to bare metal and all components and wiring were reconditioned or replaced; their turret assemblies were completely rebuilt. The rejuvenated Mle 51s remained obsolescent and in 1984 a study was conducted to decide either to replace the AMX13s with more modern vehicles or to upgrade them substantially. This concluded that the upgrade option was more cost effective (by about 80 per cent) and the Singapore AMX13 modernization programme was authorized.[59]

Through 1985 until October 1986 two prototypes with different diesel powertrains were built and trialled extensively to determine the choice. The two options were either a foreign kit with semi-automatic transmission or SAE's own kit with a fully automatic transmission. The Singapore Army eventually selected the SAE kit and the upgrade package was accepted for service as the AMX13 SM1 or simply SM1. The old SOFAM petrol engine was replaced with a Detroit Diesel 6V-53T engine and modernizations included the ZF 5WG-180 automatic

View of a Singaporean AMX13 Mle 51 which had just smashed through an obstacle during a public display on the grounds of the Changi Air Base in June 1978. This is an ex-IDF vehicle, identifiable by the searchlight bracket at the rear of the turret roof and the raised turret ring platform upon which the turret was seated. (*Lam Chun See*)

The stowage on the turret exterior of a typical Singaporean Mle 51 (until the introduction of the AMX13 SM1) consisted of a dual jerry can holder, a 7.62mm machinegun tripod holder, and an open-top box for carrying four 7.62mm ammunition boxes. The stowage design (less the tripod holder) originated from the ex-IDF Mle 51s and the Singaporeans retrofitted it onto their other Mle 51s acquired from Switzerland (like the one in this picture) and India. (*Peter Lau Collection*)

Before the introduction of the indigenous Bionix IFV, the AMX13 attracted much public attention (including the teenage Peter Lau who wore a red cap in this 1988 photo) as it represented the might of the Singapore Armoured Forces. Based on the emblem painted onto the cover of the spare road wheel, this vehicle belonged to the School of Armour (SOA). (*Lau Ah Bah / Peter Lau Collection*)

Sadly the pioneer tank of the Singapore Armed Forces was all but forgotten by the public after the acquisition of the Leopard 2 MBT. Nonetheless an original Mle 51 with Type 2C chassis was featured as an exhibit during a 2012 exhibition which commemorated the 45th anniversary of Singapore's National Service. It should be noted that the camouflage net was not draped correctly on this vehicle; the right way would be that of the SOA tank in the previous picture.

The AMX-13 SM1s that were upgraded from ex-Swiss Army vehicles retained some of their unique Swiss features such as the slanted grab handles at the rear of the turret and the spare tracks stowed on the lower rear of the hull below the towing hitch. (*Mike Yeo*)

An AMX-13 SM1 on a National Day parade rehearsal in 2005. The reworked hull front, hydro-pneumatic suspensions, raised turret platform and the turret side baskets can be seen clearly. (*Mike Yeo*)

The petite AMX13 SM1 was highly manoeuvrable and adequately armed for closed terrain operations but its combat effectiveness was eroded when the PT-91 MBT was introduced into the region. The picture here shows a SM1 from the 41st Battalion Singapore Armoured Regiment in 2004. The visible markings include the unit's logo at both sides of the turret, the vehicle number and a yellow bridging disc on the left fender. (*Peter Lau*)

The AMX-13 SM1 Launched Bridge (SLB) was converted from redundant Mle 51 gun tanks by ST Kinetics (then ST Automotive), and it served with field engineer battalions. It carried a twin-treadway assault bridge that extended to 15 metres with a width of 3.2 metres. (*Mike Yeo*)

Rear right view of the SLB showing its rear-mounted auxiliary power unit. The vehicle has a pair of stabilizers located at its front which are deployed during bridge laying operations. Note the rubber-padded tracks, "holed" idler wheels and foot-steps welded to the rear fenders.

transmission, a new electrical system, and the adoption of the 'Dunlopstrut' hydro-pneumatic suspension. In the turret the original telescopic gunner's sight was replaced by a modern electro-optical day/night sight with fire control capability. This in turn enabled the firing of the newly-developed 75mm APFSDS-T rounds from the Charter Industries of Singapore (CIS).[60]

In September 1987, the upgrade programme commenced at SAE (subsequently renamed Singapore Technologies Kinetics or ST Kinetics). On 15 June 1988, the first SM1 rolled off the production line and was officially commissioned at a ceremony held at SAE's Portsdown Road plant. The SM1 remained the most numerous and most heavily armed tank in the Peninsula until the 2007 introduction of the Malaysian PT91 MBT. To address the imbalance in capability with the PT91, Singapore resolved to buy the Leopard 2 A4 MBT in 2006. Because deliveries were expected in 2008, it was deemed necessary to improve the SM1s until they could pass the torch to the 'big cats'. As a result, ST Kinetics was awarded a last AMX13 related contract in 2005. The SLEP (Service Life Extension Programme) ensured the continued operability of a portion of the AMX13 fleet until retirement. Meanwhile the drawdown of the AMX13 SM1 fleet began on 31 October 2006 when the first batch of sixteen decommissioned SM1s was scrapped. The last AMX13 SM1 tanks were finally deactivated in 2011.[61]

Apart from AMX13 SM1 light tank, the SAF also operated a locally modified bridge layer version of the SM1. This was the AMX13 SM1-Launched Bridge (SLB) which joined the Singapore Combat Engineers in 1992. This two-man crewed vehicle was based on the chassis of the SM1 tank and carried a folding bridge that could be deployed in 15 minutes to cross gaps of 14 metres. Although not widely known, a troop carrier variant of the AMX13 SM1 also existed as a private venture developed by Singapore Technology Automotive for the export market. In 1994 a single prototype of an upgraded AMX13 VCI was completed with the same power pack and hydropneumatic suspension units as the AMX13 SM1 light tank. The vehicle was armed with the CIS designed 40/50 weapon station (mounting the CIS 40mm automatic grenade launcher and a CIS 12.7mm heavy machine gun) which was also employed on the upgraded M113s and the Bionix 40/50 infantry fighting vehicles of the Singapore army.[62]

While the Indonesian Army's fleet of AMX based recovery vehicles, armoured personnel carriers and self-propelled guns have been kept in near original configuration their Mle 51 and Mle 58 tanks underwent a retrofit programme at the Bengpuspalad Central Equipment Workshop to bring them roughly up to Singaporean SM1 standard. The upgrade was accomplished in 1995 with kits supplied by Singapore Technologies Automotive but did not include the upgraded gunner's sight. The total number of upgraded tanks is unconfirmed but Indonesia still has around 400 AMX13 vehicles in service in 2016.[63]

France kept a small force of AMX13s in use into the early 1990s in Djibouti, many or all of which were later gifted to local allies. The French presence in strategically positioned Djibouti increased after the Algerian war ended in the 1960s. French intervention elsewhere in Africa has also continued – usually in support of local allies. The 1976 'loan' of 5 AMX13 C90s to the Ivorian forces to dissuade aggression from Guinea by the *4e Batallion d'Infanterie de Marine* (4e BIMA, later the 43e BIMA) stationed at Abidjan was neither the first nor last transfer of French weapons as 'aid' in Africa. Djibouti acquired some sixty Mle 51 or AMX13 C90s by the same means in 1978; Tunisia and Morocco may both have received gifts of second-hand AMX13s between the late 1960s and the early 1980s.

In late 1988, Venezuela contracted Creusot-Loire (by then operating with substantial help from GIAT) to supply thirty-one modernized AMX13 C90 light tanks to replace the old Mle 51s in their inventory. The company stripped down and rebuilt the former French Army vehicles at about half the price of the same number of new tanks. The old SOFAM engine was replaced with a Detroit Diesel 6V-53T engine coupled to a Borg Warner three-speed fully automatic transmission with torque converter; a new Chausson air-water/oil cooler with a thermostatically-controlled centrifugal fan, a 200A generator and NATO 6TN batteries were also fitted. The torsion bar suspension was replaced with hydropneumatic units for improved cross-country mobility. Turret updates included the installation of a SOPELEM 18-02 SOPTAC fire-control system with a M213 day sight and a TCV-107 laser rangefinder, replacement of the coaxial weapon with a 7.62mm AA-52 NF-1 machine gun, installation of an Israeli *Tadiran* frequency-hopping radio and a revised intercom system. Deliveries of the tanks to Venezuela took place between 1988 and late 1990. The old Mle 51s were decommissioned and put into storage as the rebuilt vehicles arrived.[64]

Mexico has become a significant user of second-hand AMX13 VTT Mle 56s. In 1994 Mexico bought 268 AMX13 series vehicles from a Belgian dealer, reportedly including 136 tanks. It is probable that the tanks are ex-French C90s that could have been part of a package purchase

Venezuela contracted Creusot-Loire to supply 31 overhauled and modernized AMX13 C90s to replace their antiquated Mle 51s in late 1988. These ex-French Army vehicles were rebuilt to the latest standards at half the price of new tanks. (*Carlos Antonio Arroyo Alonso*)

The update to the chassis comprised a new Detroit Diesel 6V-53T engine coupled to a Borg Warner automatic transmission, a new air-water/oil cooler, a 200A generator, NATO 6TN batteries and a new hydropneumatic suspension system. For the turret, the SOPELEM 18-02 SOTAC fire control system was installed together with a new 7.62mm AA-52-NF-1 coaxial machinegun, Tadiran frequency-hopping radio and a revised intercom system. (*Collection Danter César*)

A Mexican DNC-1 with CAFL38 machine-gun turret on maneuvers. It was understood that the DNC-1s had been retrofitted with diesel engines. Externally the DNC-1 can be differentiated from the original VTT Mle 56s by a few features: an additional grille above the three original ones at the right corner slope of the superstructure, a wire mesh guard for the exhaust, and a hinged top cover for the engine compartment. Note the two hinges at the lower right side of the superstructure. (*Andrés Tonini*)

of surplus VTT Mle 56s. The AMX13 C90s have reportedly been stored (either as a spares source or until they are modernized or sold). At present Mexico does not operate tanks, relying on the ERC 90 as its most powerfully armed AFV. It is likely that most of the Mexican VTTs came from former French stocks. The Mexican Army has eight *Regimentos Mecanizados* in its order of battle and visual evidence points towards their possession of a large fleet of VTT Mle 56s (including versions armed with the CAFL38 machine gun turret, the S470 12.7mm cupola, and the modernized VTT Mle 56 T20-13). The total number of Mexican AMX13 Mle 56 VTTs is thought to be around 400 vehicles and are designated DNC 1.[65]

Chapter Fourteen

Modernizing the AMX13

In the third world the Mle 51 and Mle 58 have served many armies as a main battle tank for decades. Often the countries that bought the AMX13 could not afford to re-equip their forces for many years and several armies have chosen to modernize their Mle 51s and Mle 58s. Modernizations have resulted in the AMX13 being converted to new roles or have simply extended the AMX13's service life in the battle tank role. Even at the time of writing in 2016 significant opportunities exist for component modernization that can be combined into comprehensive upgrades for the AMX13 fleets in use in Asia and in South America. The

The Venezuelan AMX13 Mle 51 seen here has served as a test bed for alternative powerplants. It has possibly been fitted with a Deutz diesel engine in a very similar configuration to that seen on upgraded Argentinian and Ecuadorean vehicles. (*Collection Danter César*)

The tracked Venezuelan LAR-160 system has good cross country mobility which enables it to follow the armoured columns. Its 160mm rockets has a 40kg HE-COFRAM warhead and a maximum range of 30km. Once all rockets are fired, the reloading operation can be accomplished in 10 minutes using one of the crane-equipped trucks in the background to remove and replace the rocket pods. (*Claude Dubary*)

adaptation of the Mle 58's 105mm gun to fire newer French 105mm ammunition types and the use of laser range finding equipment and thermal sights have been significant in many turret modernizations. The AMX13's lethal range has been extended and its mechanical performance improved to approach the standards seen in more modern AFVs.

Local ingenuity and imagination have driven comprehensive modifications to the AMX13. In 1983, Venezuela ordered twenty-five AMX13 based LAR-160 Light Artillery Rocket System from Israeli Military Industries Ltd. The system consists of an AMX13 light tank chassis fitted with the Detroit Diesel 6V-53T diesel engine, with the turret replaced by a rocket launcher mounting two launcher pods with eighteen 160mm rockets each. The LAR-160s entered service in 1984 and equipped two batteries of the No.1 Multiple Rocket Launcher Artillery Group *"General en Jefe José Gregorio Monagas"* (later retitled 103 Artillery Group). The system remained in service until the mid-2000s when it was replaced by the more conventional Russian BM-21 "Grad" truck-mounted 122mm multiple rocket launcher system.[66]

In 1996, the Venezuelan Armour Maintenance Centre (CEMANBLIN) modified one of its decommissioned Mle 51 tanks to mount a twin 20mm SAMM S530 turret taken from a Panhard AML-S530 that had been in storage since 1983. The resulting prototype *Aguijón*

A pair of modernized Ecuadorian AMX13 Mle 58s awaits the commencement of the annual *Batalla de Pichincha* parade on 24th May 2012. The upgrades are hardly noticeable when viewed from this angle except for the new muzzle brake, headlight assemblies and the raised right sponson. The upgraded gun closely follows the CN-105-G1 standard, with the capability of firing APFSDS type ammunition. The muzzle brake is probably identical to that developed for the AMX10RC reconnaissance vehicle. (*Jorge G. Aguirre*)

Side view of the modernized Ecuadorian Mle 58. Note the pair of hinges welded to the top edge of the engine access cover. (*Jorge G. Aguirre*)

(Stinger) air defence vehicle underwent trials but further conversions did not result because it failed to meet expectations. Two years later another attempt to create air defence vehicles from redundant Mle 51 hulls by mounting turrets from derelict M42 Dusters in storage resulted in the manufacture of seven conversions. These vehicles were known as *Rafaga* air defence vehicles and they form the air defence battery for the *General de Division Juan Jacinto Lara* field artillery group, which operates Venezuela's AM F3s. The Venezuelans have modernized the power trains of their AMX13 variants as have other South American armies. In 2003 the viability of the Deutz F8L-413F eight-cylinder diesel as a replacement engine for the VTT Mle 56 was tested by CEMANBLIN. This had already been successfully implemented by Argentina, Ecuador and Peru to modernize different AMX13 variants. In 2013 the Venezuelan army began to modernize some 300 armoured vehicles of numerous types at the CEMANBLIN facilities located at Fuerte Paramacay in Carabobo state. The rebuilt AMX13 C90s, AMX13 VTTs and the artillery's AM F3 self-propelled guns were all selected for modernization – a process that is probably still underway.[67]

By the late 1980s, component aging had begun to affect Ecuador's AMX13 availability and plans were made to replace the SOFAM petrol engine and to modernize the Mle 58's fire

The second version of the Alacrán tank destroyer as seen during the Independence Day parade in 2010. For this configuration, the number of Kornet anti-tank missile launchers was reduced from the original four tubes to two. (*Victor Torres*)

The *Alacrán* turrets were modified from the original FL12 gun turrets by the trimming of the *corps oscillant* and the plugging of the aperture for the 105mm gun. For self-defence a .50 calibre M2 Browning machinegun was fitted onto an A-frame to the front of the commander's hatch. The intended role for the vehicle is suggested by the vehicle's markings showing scorpion (*Alacrán* in Spanish) posed to sting a Leopard 2 MBT (which only Chile possessed in the whole of South America). (*Victor Torres*)

control system. The Ecuadorian army decided to install the French SOPELEM SOPTAC 18-04 fire control system, which comprised a laser rangefinder and ballistic computer. The 105mm gun was modified to fire 105mm OFL (*Obus Flèche* or APFSDS) rounds by changing the double-baffle muzzle brake of the 105mm gun to a single-baffle muzzle brake and by modifying the automatic loader. The installation of the SOPTAC 18 system began during late 1988 and was completed in 1990. The first round hit probability of the modified vehicles was increased significantly and permitted use of the more lethal APFSDS rounds developed for the 105mm gun in France in the late 1970s. At the same time the engine replacement issue was examined; new power train options from various firms were examined and one French solution was tested unsuccessfully in Ecuador. A project by the ESPE (Ecuadorian Armed Forces University) followed to modernize the AMX13 series engines. The goal was to prolong the service life of the vehicles, improve reliability under extreme conditions and improve battlefield mobility using a commercially available diesel that could be supported locally. A German-made Deutz

The reworked hull front of the Indonesian Pindad upgraded Mle 58 houses its new 400hp Navistar diesel engine. This demonstrator vehicle's FL12 turret carries a prominent appliqué armour array and the 105mm barrel thermal sleeve developed for the Austrian SK105 – the likely source for its upgraded turret. (*Dicky Asmoro, ARC Inc.*)

The side skirts and the new smoke dischargers add to the Pindad upgraded Mle 58's very modern appearance. The adaptation of available technology to maintain the combat viability of the AMX13 seen here is one of the most radical ever attempted on the AMX13 platform. It is uncertain how many vehicles will be modified to this standard. (*Dicky Asmoro, ARC Inc.*)

The left side of the Pindad modernized hull and the altered profile of the late model FL12 turret are clearly visible. (*Dicky Asmoro, ARC Inc.*)

The rear of the vehicle's hull has changed little except for the new rear lights. We can see the stowage arrangement for the rear tarp carrier and for the spare track links carried on the rear plate. (*Dicky Asmoro, ARC Inc.*)

A side view of the less radical of the Pindad modernized AMX13s, based on former KL Mle 58s and similar in some ways to the SM1. The upgraded suspension is clearly visible. (*Dicky Asmoro, ARC Inc.*)

A thermal imaging (TI) camera is mounted on the glacis plate in front of the driver's periscopes to improve the night driving capability. During night operations the image from the TI camera is displayed on a LCD screen at the driver's station. (*Dicky Asmoro, ARC Inc.*)

The AMX13 has served the Indonesian army for many years; its size and weight make it particularly suited to the Indonesian cavalry's requirements. (*Dicky Asmoro, ARC Inc.*)

Despite the Indonesian government's intention to purchase a heavier MBT the topography there makes modernization of the AMX13 a very attractive proposition. A light vehicle with respectable fire power and good cross-country performance at similar cost has yet to emerge – at least in a form fitting their army's requirements. (*Dicky Asmoro, ARC Inc.*)

diesel engine was adapted in collaboration with the workshops of the Army Corps of Engineers and financially-sponsored by the Ecuadorean private sector based on risk reversal agreements. Development was completed in 1990 and all objectives were achieved at only a third of the cost of foreign solutions. The ESPE solution was approved for fleet implementation with the upgrades being performed by technicians of the CEMAB (Armour Maintenance Centre), and was completed in mid-2001.[68]

Between 2008 and 2010 Peru rebuilt twenty-four AMX13s into AMX13 *Alacrán* missile-armed tank destroyers to increase the army's antitank capabilities against Chilean Leopard 2A4s. Each new AMX13 *Alacrán* tank destroyer was based on a hull already fitted with the F8L-413F Deutz 240 HP engine. In all four variations on the *Alacrán* design have been identified, probably as a result of incremental design improvements or due to systems availability. The conversion required the basic Mle 58 hull to be completely stripped down. All bearings, hydraulics and electrical systems were replaced and the power train was overhauled. The turret was reworked and the main gun dismantled; the resulting new missile turret designed by SMGE (War Material Project Service) was installed with an external mounting for two 9M113 Kornet-E anti-tank missiles and a mounting for the Kornet's 1PN79-1 guidance and targeting system. The fire controls include a thermal viewer to permit night operation and all weather capability. The AMX13 *Alacrán* mounts a Browning M-2 HB 12.7 mm on a pintle mounting on the left side of the turret with 500 rounds. The turret houses the fire control electronics and four reloads. All the conversions were undertaken in Peru using missiles with fire controls sourced in Russia.[69]

The AMX13 PA8 *Escorpion 2* is a less radical Peruvian optimization of the Mle 58 similar to the old AMX13 SS11. It is fitted with the Dante fire control system (incorporating a laser rangefinder and thermal vision) and mounts two Ukrainian R2 Barrier antitank guided missiles on the turret rear and with the missile's guidance system and fire controls. The missiles serve as a complimentary armament to the 105mm gun for engaging modern MBT targets. The 105mm gun and automatic loading system was modified to fire APFSDS-T ammunition and the commander and gunner's station have been equipped with pintle mounted machine guns. The total number converted is possibly around thirty vehicles.

In 2011, PT Pindad was awarded a contract to modernize the Indonesian TNI's AMX13 Mle 58 tanks as part of the Indonesian government's strategy for defence self-reliance (a component of the Minimum Essential Force programme). The retrofit project began at the end of 2011, but the actual vehicle modification only commenced in 2013. The first prototype was, after many challenges, eventually completed in early 2014 and presented to the Deputy Defence Minister on 26 March 2014. The prototype was subjected to a series of mobility trials at the area of Sukabumi and Cianjur and firing tests in April 2014 with 105mm HE and APFSDS ammunition. The first thirteen conversions were delivered to *Yonkav 2/Tank* on 7 October 2014 along with the army's newly commissioned Leopard 2 and Marder IFVs for the TNI's 69th anniversary parade.[70]

The Pindad retrofit involved major changes to both the chassis and the turret. The front of the hulls were rebuilt (and extended by about 20 cm) to accommodate a new Navistar diesel power train. The original FL12 turrets were replaced with late pattern FL12 turrets which appear identical to those employed on the SK105 *Kürassier*. A new Belgian fire control system is reportedly fitted to increase the effectiveness of the 105mm CN 105 G1 gun. The retrofitting of the rest of the TNI's AMX13 fleet was scheduled between 2015 and 2019; further conversions remain unfulfilled at the time of writing.

Chapter Fifteen

The AMX13 Mle 51 as a Combat Vehicle

The AMX 13 saw combat both in conventional warfare and in low intensity actions against guerilla forces. As a combat vehicle it had advantages and limitations that determined how it was best used and it was generally liked by its crews. The AMX13 Mle 51 had a road speed of 60 km/h and a range of nearly 400 km on roads – far better than most NATO medium tanks of the time (particularly given the use of a petrol engine). In the 1950s the Mle 51's fire power was superior to any other light tank and the most common medium tank then in French service – the M4 Sherman series. The AMX13 C90 and Mle 58 perpetuated the Mle 51's impressive firepower in the following decade. The AMX13 was popular with its crews for the power of its gun and for its manoeuvrability. Its inherent disadvantages resulted from the necessary design trade-offs that allowed the mounting of such a powerful gun in such a small vehicle. The tank's size placed limitations on crewmen's height and limited engine and transmission component accessibility. Throughout its long service life the AMX13's suspension was regarded as relatively fragile and its tracks required regular adjustment. The gear changing matrix was tricky for the driver to master, and drivers needed to be mindful of the turret's traverse to avoid serious injury. The triangular head guard introduced for the driver during production was a direct result of serious accidents.[71]

The FL10 turret lacked a gun stabilisation system and the AMX13 was expected to fire from the short halt. In 1952 this was not a huge drawback because stabilised gun systems were only just beginning to be introduced; in the French Army this particular design feature was accorded a lower priority than in the US or British armies. In later years this became more serious as it delayed target acquisition when was not fighting from ambush positions. Its automatic loading system allowed the AMX13 a very high rate of fire but it also ran short of ready rounds very quickly. Although the commander could load the main gun manually when the autoloader's magazines were emptied (or in case of emergency) the tank could be rendered ineffective because this was a slow process. The commander also risked rapidly losing his situational awareness if he spent any length of time serving as a loader.

To keep full combat effectiveness, the two autoloader drums had to be reloaded externally. One crewman had to dismount and stand on the turret while the others passed him the stowed rounds from within or from the ground. This process was risky on any kind of contested ground but could be accomplished a few rounds at a time as long as the ammunition racks held out. A complete restocking of all the vehicle ammunition racks took about two hours as the inaccessibility of the ammunition racks in the hull required multiple traverses of the turret. Unpacking the original 75mm rounds from carefully packed wooden cases also added to replenishment time; reloading, therefore, always needed careful planning and execution in a secure area with a covering force in place.[72]

An important limitation of the Mle 51 as a combat weapon against infantry was the inability of the autoloader system to handle high explosive rounds (which the commander had to load manually) and the small amount of coaxial machine-gun ammunition carried. The Mle 51 only carried 900 rounds of such ammunition versus 3,750 and 2,280 rounds stowed on the M24 Chaffee and EBR respectively. The 75mm (and later 90mm and 105mm) armour piercing rounds had a pointed nose that slid easily into the gun breech from the autoloader tray, whereas high explosive rounds were fused and presented serious risks loading with the automatic rammer (and a very real risk of high explosive rounds detonating if the round fouled the edge of the breech block instead of the chamber). The use of 75mm high explosive ammunition for range practice using the CN 75-50 in the French Army was a rarity in peacetime. In practice, from its earliest trials, the French found that the ideal use of the Mle 51 was as a tank destroyer.[73]

The following remarks were extracted from the document provided for the Saumur reserve Calvary officer course (cycle 1955-56), noting the vehicle's principal attributes and the logical conclusion for how it was intended to be employed by the *Arme Blindée Cavalerie*:

The tank can be equipped with the FL 11 turret of the E.B.R. This lightens the weight by 1.5 tonnes.

The following have emerged from the study of the 13 tonnes tank:

- Excellent anti-tank capability of the 75mm cannon carried by the 13 tonne tank attributed to penetration power, accuracy and high rate of fire.
- Low ammunition provision for the 13 tonne tank, with only 12 ready rounds in the autoloader drums. In addition, the provisioned machine gun ammunition (900 rounds) makes this tank unfit for contact, attack, and exploitation missions.
- Weak armour that puts the 13 tonnes tank at the mercy of **all** heavy weapons. The 13 tonnes tank is more specifically suited to fulfill missions of 'tank destroyer'.[74]

The Mle 51 was designed to be crewed by men of average height in 1947, when most Frenchmen were 170-172cm tall. Commanders could be taller but the AMX13 was uncomfortable for a big man. Taller drivers and gunners found difficulty contorting themselves to suit the tank's dimensions and crewmen were chosen according to their size. Due to the discomforts of the hull and fighting compartment the crew could not man the vehicle if it was closed down for extended periods – and the layout of its controls precluded the AMX13 operating as a combat vehicle without its full crew. Crewmen used to the comforts of the M24 found the AMX13 to be cramped and often emerged from cross country operation covered in bruises. Former crewmen comparing the M24 and AMX13 Mle 51 have described the Chaffee as 'palatial' in comparison to the spartan French tank. Additionally there was no

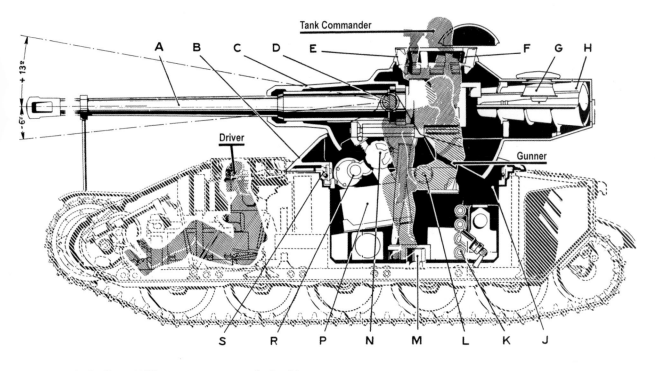

A - Gun, 75mm, model 1950
B - Rotating (traversing) unit of the turret
C - Oscillating (elevating) unit of the turret
D - Trunnion
E - Episcope
F - Commander's cupola

G - Air ventilator
H - (Ammunition) Magazine drums
J - Turret basket
K - Rear ammunition rack
L - Turret traverse lock
M - Slip ring

N - Elevating hand wheel
P - Radio set
R - Elevating gear
S - Turret ring

FL. 10 TURRET (OVERVIEW)

The crew positions in the AMX13 are so limited in space that even the smaller-sized Asians found them uncomfortable to operate in. (*Thomas Seignon*)

crew compartment heater and Mle 51's oscillating turret design was completely impractical for sealing the vehicle even while shallow wading; it leaked like a sieve in rain.[75]

The AMX13 had a relatively reliable engine and transmission but was much noisier than the M24. Their tactical suitability was questionable when used as reconnaissance vehicles (as the Mle 58 was employed in the Netherlands army). Dutch complaints about reliability may have been aggravated by the restrictions on annual mileage and the lack of facilities for exercises in the Netherlands. The same may have applied elsewhere. Smaller armies kept their AMX13s of all types operational for decades after they were retired by NATO. Crews frequently complained about the bumpy ride; the suspensions of the Mle 51 Series 1 and Series 2A were stiff and their torsion bars and shock absorbers were not adjustable. Modifications to the AMX13's suspension were first implemented on the 2D chassis, and some of these were subsequently propagated to the earlier hulls under the 2R upgrade programme. The type 2A, 2B and 2C chassis all had the same basic running gear design and the modification to the track support roller seen on the Type 2D chassis was necessary to allow the integration of the new rotary shock absorber.

AMX13 Mle 51 tanks of the 20 Lancers at Chushul during the 1962 Sino-India border war. The chassis of the tanks are of Type 2C as evident by the horizontal covers of the lateral stowage bins and the two support rollers for the tracks. These vehicles were stripped for air transport; frequent mechanical issues occurred in this action due to the high altitude and freezing temperatures – which might explain why the access covers have been removed from the glacis on both vehicles. (*United Service Institute of India*)

Overall the AMX13's performance as a combat vehicle has to be weighed in context of when it was fighting, and, as it constantly evolved, the version being employed.

The Indian Army made good use of the Mle 51 in the 1962 border incident with China and again against Pakistan in 1965. In 1962 the Indians gave the tank its first and only taste of war as an air portable weapon; 2 troops of AMX13s (6 tanks) from the 20th Lancers were hastily dispatched to reinforce the 114th Infantry Brigade as the Chinese threat to the Chushul sector became imminent. The tanks were carried to the Chandigarh airbase on tank transporters; from there the AN-12s of the IAF's 44th Squadron would airlift them to the 4,300m high Chushul airstrip in the Himalayas. The loading of the first tank on 22 October 1962 was unsuccessful because of damage to the floor of the aircraft during loading; the tank tipped hard after it had climbed the steep ramp into the aircraft and its tracks slipped on the aluminum floor of the aircraft. To resolve the issue a loading platform was devised and constructed overnight, along with a suitable ramp, and the floor of the aircraft was covered with wooden planks. The platform was made flush with the floor of the aircraft and the tank was driven smoothly into the aircraft while the wood-decking of the cargo hold provided a positive gripping surface for its tracks; a successful loading was achieved by noon on 24 October.

The weight of the loaded aircraft was also a major concern because the all-up weight far exceeded the AN-12's limit for takeoff. The Air Force initially insisted that the tank gun, if not

Israeli OB 105 AUs bombarding Egyptian positions on the northern sector of the Suez Canal during the 1967 Six-Day War. (*Han Micha / Israel Government Press Office*)

The amount of ammunition stockpiled behind the battery and the proximity of the vehicle to each other suggests that these Israeli OB 015 AUs are laying a barrage with little fear of air attack. Note the Browning M1919 .30 calibre machine gun on the gun commander's cupola. (*Han Micha / Israel Government Press Office*)

An Israeli armoured unit equipped with Mle 51s photographed shortly after entering Gaza during the Six Day War in 1967. (*Milner Moshe/Israeli Government Press Office*)

The AMX13 could not absorb the kind of punishment that one could expect from heavier opponents and it relied on solid reconnaissance and tactical awareness in order to get in a first shot. If it was hit and penetrated, the ammunition and gasoline stored in the rear end of the vehicle and in the automatic loader would explode with catastrophic results. (*Harel Yehuda/ Israeli Government Press Office*)

An Israeli M50 unit advances past a knocked out Mle 51 on the Golan Heights in 1967. (*Harel Yehuda/ Israeli Government Press Office*)

An IDF mechanic repairing battle damage sustained at the final drive area of an IDF Mle 51 on the Golan Heights in 1967. It can be seen that the shot had glanced off the edge of the transmission housing into the final drive. (*Milner Moshe/Israeli Government Press Office*)

The crew of an IDF Mle 51 enjoying a moment of peace during a lull in the fighting in the 1967 war. The photo shows that the tank was equipped with the triangular head protector. (*Kutin Assaf / Israel Government Press Office*)

the whole turret, be removed prior to loading and that it should be reassembled at Chushul. They relented once they learnt of the enemy's proximity to the airfield and the obvious need for the tanks to be operational within the shortest time possible after landing. To meet the minimum takeoff weight, both the aircraft and the Mle 51s were subjected to weight reductions. The aircraft's fuel was cut down to the barest minimum required for the two-way journey and a short stay at the airfield without switching off the engines. The tanks had all ammunition unloaded, minimum fuel, and all detachable plates, equipment and stowage items removed. The first tank troop commenced loading on the night of the 24-25 October. In the early morning of 25 October the first AN-12 left Chandigarh to deliver its tank while the others waited with orders to follow one at a time upon its successful return to base. The day's airlift proceeded without a hitch; the remaining tank troop was loaded that night and by the noon on the 26 October all six tanks had been successfully airlifted to Chushul.[76]

The Mle 51's mission in the Himalayas was to deny the Spanggur Gap approach to the enemy, particularly to any Chinese armour that may try to venture out towards Chushul. It was to act as a mobile reserve with an infantry company to safeguard the flanks of the brigade and against sizeable infiltrations along the Tsaka La-Chushul road. It was also to provide close fire support to the Indian infantry. The area to the west of the Chushul airfield was the most ideal for deploying the tanks to meet a Chinese armour assault through the Spanggur Gap. As they were in the centre of the Brigade's sector the tanks could also mount rapid counter attacks in conjunction with infantry if required. Any deployment in the area could, however, be seen by the Chinese artillery observation posts and the tanks expected to come under artillery fire when battle commenced. It was decided that this problem could be limited by locating them in a 'hide' position at the base of the Gurung Hill and a separate position was prepared west of the airfield. During the battle, the tanks were to provide fire support to Gurung Hill while in the 'hide' position. They were to leave this when executing a counter attack or move to the prepared position west of the airfield in the event of a Chinese armoured assault.[77]

The AMX13 was not designed for high altitude operations, and the Indian tank crews soon discovered that their tanks were not performing as expected. Field innovations solved many mechanical problems. Low atmospheric pressure at high altitude created power loss and stalling; thin air enriched the fuel mixture which burned incompletely and produced less power. To resolve the problem a thin copper wire was inserted in the main jet of the carburettor by field technicians to reduce the flow of the fuel. This did not restore the engine power but did minimize stalling. This experience made the French realize the necessity to develop a suitable turbocharger for the SOFAM 8 Gxb engine.

The tanks proved difficult to start in the sub-zero temperatures. A temporary solution was to keep one tank engine running to permit the rest of the troop to be slave started by connecting their female socket with jumper lead from the one running engine. The tanks' engines also encountered problems building up their operating temperature due to the low boiling point of water at high altitude. On 17 November an engineer of the TDEV tried to resolve this by fitting a higher rating vapour pressure relief valve to a vehicle's water header tank. Unfortunately the Chinese attacked in the early morning of 18 November and the unproven vapour pressure relief valve caused the header tank of this vehicle to burst and one tank was immobilized!

The subsequent career of the AMX13 in the 1965 war against Pakistan is generally considered to have been successful in a number of battles in which it was correctly used; exact details, however, are very hard to discern amongst the highly disputed claims made by both sides. British intelligence documents from attachés allowed to inspect the battlefields indicated that the 75mm was capable of penetrating the Pakistani M47 Patton.[78]

The need to up-gun the Mle 1951 by the mid-1960s was proven decisively two years later in the battles for the Sinai passes fought by Lieutenant-Colonel Zeev Eitan's 19th Light Tank Battalion during the 1967 Arab-Israeli war. By this time the Mle 51 was no longer capable of defeating the latest Soviet MBTs in the Egyptian and Syrian arsenals, although it performed well in several crucial engagements against Jordanian M48s. The 6 Day War marked the swan song of the AMX 13 Mle 51 in Israeli service.

The diminutive AMX13s engaged the enemy with their 75mm guns but saw their armour-piercing shells bounce off the T-55s frontal armour while the enemy's heavier tank guns replied, knocking out some of the Israeli unit's half-tracks and light tanks with ease. One of these was laden with ammunition and exploded, which then set off a chain reaction destroying a further seven half-tracks and a tank, killing 16 Israelis. The battle continued with the much lighter Israeli tanks faring badly, until the CO personally led some of his tanks off to a flank to engage the thinner side armour of the enemy AFVs. The battle lasted for some two hours when, eventually, the light tanks were forced to withdraw for want of fuel and ammunition. Fortunately at this time, a battalion of upgraded M51 Sherman tanks, mounting the 105mm L/44 gun, arrived to even up the odds.[79]

A Cambodian AMX13 Mle 51 of the FANK Armoured Brigade with .50 calibre M2 Browning machine gun. This tank may have been attached to the 13th (Tiger) Brigade (commanded by Prince Norodom Chantaraingsey) to which Spencer Dale (in front of the tank) had been allowed access. The heavy machine gun was probably fitted to husband FANK's supply of 75mm ammunition, which had dropped to critical levels in 1971. (*Spencer Dale, with thanks to Mike Brown*)

From the handful of photographs available the Cambodian Mle 51s appeared to be vehicles with late production turrets on Type 2A-2R chassis. (*Spencer Dale, with thanks to Mike Brown*)

The AMX 13 was used successfully in counterinsurgency operations by several of the world's smaller armies. During the *El Porteñazo* coup attempt in Venezuela in June 1962, sixteen AMX13 Mle 51 tanks from the *Bravos de Apure* participated in the operation to recapture Puerto Cabello city from the military rebels. The close-quarter fire support rendered by the AMX13s was invaluable to the loyalist infantry thrusting into the city as insurgent positions were easily demolished by the Mle 51's 75mm gun.

During the 1965 Dominican Civil War the AMX13s were deployed by the Military Junta to assault and recapture the capital city of Santo Domingo on 26 April. Two AMX13s were subsequently captured by rebels and were sent to attack the Police headquarters and to assault the Ozama Fortress, a major armoury. To distinguish the tanks they had captured the rebels embellished them with the word 'Pueblo' (People). With the rapidly deteriorating Dominican situation the U.S. initiated Operation Power Pack to evacuate American citizens and to prevent the establishment of another Communist state in its backyard. In the ensuing deployment, an M50 Ontos of the 6th U.S. Marine Expeditionary Unit knocked out two rebel tanks (a Landsverk L-60 and an AMX13) in one engagement. The L-60 was completely destroyed while the AMX13 only lost its turret. A second AMX13 was abandoned by the rebels in the same encounter and captured by the marines.[80]

In 1967 the Dominican AMX13 tanks were transferred, together with the entire armoured battalion of the CEFA, to the Combat Support Command. Little more was done to upgrade the fleet apart from the fitting of modern communications equipment to some of the AMX13 and L-60 tanks. In 1972 the AMX13 damaged by the U.S. Marines during the Civil War was modified to become the first Dominican mobile anti-aircraft vehicle. An old triple-barrelled Hispano-Suiza HS.804 20mm anti-aircraft gun was installed upon the turret-less chassis and this vehicle was known as the MAC LRC AAA. It remained in service until 2004. In 1982 the Dominican government signed an agreement with a Dutch company to exchange at least 12 operational AMX13s for surplus M41 tanks. The two remaining Mle 51s were kept in service until 2002.

The Mle 51 was also used in Cambodia's civil war against communist guerillas in the late 1960s. In 1964, the Royal Khmer Army received between twenty and forty second hand Mle 51s from France (depending on the sources) and these formed one of the tank battalions in the *Khmer Demi Brigade Blindé*. The brigade was engaged in combat for the first time in April 1967 in clearing operations against Khmer Rouge guerillas. In November 1969 Prince Sihanouk ordered a limited military campaign against North Vietnamese logistic bases in the Mondol Kiri and Ratana Kiri provinces, supported by M24 and AMX13 tanks. Cambodia became a pro-Western republic in March 1970 and within days of the change in government; the newly re-christened Forces Armées Nationale Khmere (FANK) went into action against the rebels. The Khmer Armoured Brigade led a combined task force to engage communist forces near Boret, 90 miles southeast of Phnom Penh. The unsuccessful fighting resulted in a FANK withdrawal from the border area. In August 1970 Operation "Chenla" supported by the Armoured Brigade's AMX13s was launched in order to reopen Route 6.

In 1971, the Khmer Armoured Brigade ran short of French parts and began to cannibalize their remaining AMX13s. In April 1971 FANK launched Operation 'Chenla II' to open all of Route 6 and to secure the road between Kompong Cham and Kompong Thom. The rapid advance drove the communists back and Route 6 was retaken in two weeks. Success, however, was short-lived; the PAVN counterattacked and routed the FANK task force although the armored vehicles retreated in good order toward Phnom Penh. In 1972 FANK armor was used in a series of hit-and-run operations around Phnom Penh and to keep the Mekong corridor open. In July a FANK task force joined with an ARVN armoured column to relieve the besieged city of Kompong Trabeck in the only engagement in which Khmer and South Vietnamese armored units operated together.

From January to June 1973 the Khmer Armored Brigade deployed its units north of Phnom Penh to counter the Khmer Rouge offensive. The AMX13s proved to be decisive on many occasions but combat attrition and the lack of spare parts began seriously to reduce the effectiveness of the armored battalions. By mid-1973 the Brigade had been reorganized along American lines and in early 1974 the last M24 and AMX13 tanks were withdrawn from service.[81]

The AMX13 Mle 51 and Mle 58 also saw combat in Lebanon, Africa and Central America during the 1980s in both border incidents and guerilla wars. Sadly these engagements have not been reliably enough documented for inclusion here. A common theme in most documented combat accounts remains that, while the AMX13 design was a good antitank vehicle if used correctly, it was not an ideal battle tank. Successful use depended on a good understanding of the vehicle's merits and weaknesses and on circumstances. It saw very little combat in French service but was well regarded as a combat vehicle, particularly in the era of the 5-tank platoon. French tactics were devised and refined over the following three decades to play to the strengths of the design as an important weapon in the French army's order of battle in Europe. These included the provision of range-finding detachments and organic reconnaissance capabilities at the squadron level in French AMX13 units until 1967. After the inclusion of the AMX13 SS11 in French units operating the AMX13 C90 an even more effective antitank capability was maintained for the remainder of its service. For the many other armies that purchased AMX13s training, circumstances and tactics dictated their success or failure as combat vehicles.

Accordingly, 67 years on at the time of writing, AMX13s remain in a few of the world's armouries. In its modernized forms the Mle 51 and Mle 58 are far deadlier weapons than their predecessors. They still fill a niche in the South American and Indonesian armies in the second decade of the 21st Century. The story of this family of armoured fighting vehicles will no doubt run a few more chapters and may see 70 or 75 years of service before the last are retired. It is doubtful that Messieurs Roland, Molinié, Carougeau and the other DEFA engineers who boldly advanced the AMX design would ever have dreamed that their brainchild could have lasted so long. This longevity is a tribute to the men who directed its conception and production, and to a defence industry that our more 'peaceful' world has all but extinguished in France. The AMX13 in France is an icon that reminds the French of the 40-year period of tension where a final world war seemed very near. It was also a symbol of national resurgence and its very varied crews mainly remember it with fondness for all of its strengths and weaknesses.

Notes

1. See p.25-26. Robineau, Bertrand. *Relations Internationales.* COMHART Tome 5. DGA. France. 2003. American interest in funding the 12-tonne tank under development at AMX dated from IGA Roland's visits to the USA in February 1949. Also see p.41, Kolodziej, Edward, A. *Making and Marketing Arms – The French Experience and Its Implications for the International* System, Princeton University Press. USA. 1987. By 1954, US aid as a percentage of the available military budget for weapons production and purchases amounted to over 20 per cent of the French annual defence budget

2. With characteristic modesty, Joseph Molinié set out the facts surrounding the AMX design's design and adoption in Molinié, Joseph. *Les Engins Blindés du Monde 1917-1967,* Argout-Editions, Paris, 1981.

3. See Molinié, Joseph. *Les Engins Blindés du Monde 1917-1967,* Argout-Editions, Paris, 1981. General Demetz's faith in the airborne arm and its primacy in French strategy for retaining its colonial empire suffered after the loss of Indochina in 1954.

4. See p.208. Barras. M. *L'Histoire de l'Arsenal de Roanne.* Editions Lyonnaises d'Art et d'Histoire. France, 1996. Although the requirement for air transportation was abandoned earlier, loading tests of the Mle 51 were nonetheless conducted with one of the pre-production Breguet-designed *Deux Ponts* – a later heavy lift transport design evaluated by the French air force in 1954. It is interesting to note that while the simplistic nomenclature of the new tank was embraced by the army (who called it simply *l'AMX* until the AMX30 appeared), the foreign press baptised the little tank the *Turenne* for a short time in the early 1950s. The surviving French Army technical documentation's nomenclature has been used to describe the different versions of the AMX13 in this work. In the case of the AMX13 Mle 51 light tank we have referred to the vehicle as the Mle 51 for the sake of brevity. Official nomenclature changed somewhat throughout the AMX13's career. In 1953 the documents prepared for instruction of officers in the use of the AMX13 in the CLB units (see *Notice Provisoire sur l'emploi des Petites Unités de chars de 13 T. des regiments de Cavalerie Légère Blindée.* Saumur, October 1953) tasked with reconnaissance described the AMX13 simply as the *char de 13 T. Mle 51.* A slightly later document prepared for training crews on the basics of the AMX13 Mle 51 chassis was *Le char de 13 T. 75 Mle 51 (AMX) Documentation Technique (sauf tourelle et radio), Figures.* Saumur 1955. Subsequent documents show similar subtle variations in the nomenclature of the AMX13 Mle 51 such as *char 13t-75-mle 51* seen in the *Guide d'Entretien du Char 13t-75-mle 51,* approuvé le 9 mars 1955, Edition no. 4 1959. Ministère des Armées "Terre". MAT3192. France, 1959. A much less formal description obviously in common enough use to form the official title of a 1960 tactical manual was *Char AMX.* See *Le Peloton d'AMX.* N.133. École d'Application de l'Arme Blindée et de la Cavalerie. Saumur, November 1960. The designation 'AMX-13' was widely used in foreign armies that employed the Mle 51 and Mle 58, which was usually described as a 'light tank'. In France the Mle 51 and its derivative gun-armed variants has been described as both a tank and as a tank destroyer at various times during its long career.

5. See p.66-67. Marest, Michel et Tauzin Michel. *L'Armement de Gros Calibre.* COMHART Tome 9. DGA. France. 2008. The front-engine layout was especially applicable for the design of artillery variants but would lend itself equally to the design of armoured personnel carrier versions. AMX and FCM both had considerable experience in tank design prior to the Second World War, while Batignolles-Chatillon was a company that had a long history of heavy engineering design and machine production.

6. See p.114 Marest, Michel et Tauzin Michel. *L'Armement de Gros Calibre.* COMHART Tome 9. DGA. France. 2008. Carougeau was also responsible for studying the feasibility of hollow charge 75mm rounds and discarding sabot type rounds for the CN 75-50. India also received DEFA's assistance in converting Shermans to mount the CN 75-50.

7. See Molinié, Joseph. *Les Engins Blindés du Monde 1917-1967,* Argout-Editions, Paris, 1981. Michaux was a former ARL engineer with extensive experience in AFV design. Also see p.80-81. Bruneteau, Lt-Col. *Evolution des Systemes d'Armes Sous Tourelle 1917-1995.* App. No 3789/CEAT/EF/FAS/ABC 10 April 1986. Saumur France 1986.

8. p.25-26. Robineau, Bertrand. *Relations Internationales.* COMHART Tome 5. DGA. France. 2003. Author's translation. The AMX50 was also demonstrated to the Americans at the same time. See p.44 Ibid. *"…une expérimentation à Aberdeen Proving Ground fut également organisée, en 1952, pour le prototype du char de cinquante tonnes (AMX 50), armé alors d'un canon de 100 mm à V01000 m/s. L'ingénieur militaire de 1re classe Bodin dirigeait l'équipe de l'AMX qui accompagna le matériel. Les performances du char furent plus qu'honorables, et l'AMX 50 fut systématiquement présenté aux responsables américains et étrangers, mais l'espoir d'une aide américaine pour sa production ne fut jamais concrétisé."* IGA Salmon was the director of DEFA at this time.

9. See Molinié, Joseph. *Les Engins Blindés du Monde 1917-1967,* Argout-Editions, Paris, 1981. Most sources report a relatively simple transition from prototypes to production vehicles but this reflects the basic sound design rather than

the lack of teething problems. The AMX13's early teething troubles were documented at unit level and by the STA in the 1952-53 period, see p.209. Barras. M. *L'Histoire de l'Arsenal de Roanne*. Editions Lyonnaises d'Art et d'Histoire. France, 1996. This source also notes that ARE's first production vehicles were delivered in March 1953.

10. See p.116 Robineau, Bertrand. *Relations Internationales*. COMHART Tome 5. DGA. France. 2003. SOFMA's continued position as the foreign sales agency by DTAT for GIAT was confirmed in 1970. Also see p.248-249. Mortal, Patrick. *Les Armuriers de l'Etat, du Grand Siècle à la Globalisation, 1665-1989*, Villeneuve d'Ascq, Presses Universitaires du Septentrion. France, 2007. Mortal describes 3 main production lines for the AMX13, namely the Atelier de Roanne (ARE), the Chalon sur Saonne site simply described as "Creusot-Loire" (the predecessor SFAC is not specifically named), and the La Seyne site belonging to FMC. Full tank assembly at AMX of the early production vehicles and later variants, and at Batignolles-Chatillon (BC) is not mentioned – although proven from surviving vehicle manufacturer's plates. We can presume that BC's production is counted with Creusot-Loire's as the latter company was absorbed into SFAC before it became Creusot-Loire. Turrets are listed from 3 manufacturers, Fives-Lille at Givors, Schneider at St-Etienne and Batignolles-Chatillon at Nantes. Production of turrets by SFAC is not mentioned, although evidence exists of large scale production of at a minimum 879 turrets by this firm. Mortal notes that 1482 modifications were made between the original prototype and the production Mle 51 of 1952. He notes that 7726 AMX13 series vehicles were built by 1960, 43% of which were for export. It is more likely that this total would have been completed by 1972 when production for all customers was handed over to Creusot-Loire. The best account of production and rebuilding of the AMX13 at the Atelier de Roanne is found in p.206-22. Barras. M. *L'Histoire de l'Arsenal de Roanne*. Editions Lyonnaises d'Art et d'Histoire. France, 1996. The Marne and Somme workshops at the ARE were significantly modified to produce the AMX13 in 1950. A 4km test track was also built at Roanne for testing tracked vehicles. Barras also notes that early turret batches were built at Fives-Lille. On p.212. Barras. M. *L'Histoire de l'Arsenal de Roanne*. Editions Lyonnaises d'Art et d'Histoire. France, 1996. Notes that ARE built 568 Mle 51s.

11. The Mle 51 chassis upgrades conducted prior to the major conversions of the 1960s are a controversial subject and the section that describes the matter herein is based completely on surviving documentation. The 1R upgrades were apparently applied to Series 1 vehicles only, and they are mentioned in sources dating as early as 1957. The information concerning Series 1R renovation and the 1R and 2R chassis upgrades were also made available to export customers by SOFMA in unnumbered diagrams (1R especially because Switzerland counted a number of Series 1 standard vehicles in their first AMX13 deliveries). See *Chassis AMX types 2A, 2B, 2C, 2D (et matériels remis à hauteur 1R et 2R)*. CAT. 357.726 Edition Septembre 1960. French Army *CATALOGUE de PIECES DÉTACHÉES CAT. 357.726 Edition Septembre 1960* stated that: "*Les matériels neufs, non remis à hauteur, sont différentiés entre eux par les types 2A, 2B, 2C, 2D... Par contre les types 1R et 2R définissent un mode de réparation et non pas un type unique de châssis.*" In English this states that newly built vehicles could be identified by the chassis designations of 2A, 2B, 2C and 2D while the 1R and 2R designations refer to a repair standard. The following official *Catalogue* and *Bulletin Technique* sources describe the upgrades: *Catalogue, edition de Juillet 1955, concernant le châssis type 2A complet: du Rectificatif, édition d'Avril 1956. De l'Index numérique, édition d'Octobre 1956. BT-AMX-23, édition Mars 1956, concernant la différence entre les châssis 2A, 2B et 2A, 2C. BT-AMX-26, édition de Février 1957, concernant le châssis type 1R. BT-AMX-27, édition Mars 1957, concernant le châssis type 2C. BT-AMX-28, édition Mars 1958, concernant le châssis type 2B.* These were all superseded by *CATALOGUE de PIECES DÉTACHÉES MAT. 3533 / CAT. 357.726 Edition Septembre 1960* which covered all the chassis types of the tank variant. This document recommends *BT-AMX-26, édition de Février 1957, concernant le châssis type 1R* as the source document for unmodified original parts for the Type 1R chassis. To complicate matters, Mle 51s with partial chassis upgrades toward the 2R standard were commonly referred to as 1R by the rank and file as well. Turret documentation from the same period makes no mention of changes, see *Guide d'Entretien du Char 13t – 75 – mle 51 types 2A, 2B, 2C, 2D.* The turret types mentioned are the FL.10A, FL.10A 2C, FL.10 B1 and FL. 10 D. An earlier 1957 spare part catalogue for the turret covered two turret configurations. See *CATALOGUE de PIECES DÉTACHÉES pour TOURELLE FL.10 Edition Février 1957*, which only covered FL. 10 A 2 C and FL. 10 B 1. The one snippet of evidence for turret modernization is reference to turret designation FL. 10A 2C. This could refer to an early FL. 10A turret upgraded to 2C standard but does not describe the nature of the upgrade. The FL. 10A 2C still used the original CH.2 hydraulic equipment for gun/turret laying instead of the newer CH.6 equipment used in the later FL. 10B turret. It may be that modification of the FL10 turret was left well alone until the 90mm and SS11 conversion programs.

12. The research conducted by Robert Alazet of the Amicale du 8e RH on the *8e Régiment de Hussards* during the early postwar period was of great use to our own research into the first use of this weapon in the French Army. The choice of the 8° RH as the regiment selected to test out the AMX 13 was in some regards unusual. By tradition in the French cavalry, Dragoon (*dragon*) regiments fulfilled the task of mounted skirmishers tasked with taking and holding ground, whereas Hussar (*hussard*) regiments are mounted reconnaissance units, logically suited to evaluate the EBR. The geography of the test area, Epernay, in the centre of the Champagne amid plains, wooded expanses and even the steeper country around Reims, allowed a wide range of terrain tests within a small area. We can assume that the decision to have the 8e RH evaluate both the EBR and the AMX13, in preference to a *régiment de dragons*, might have had some connection to the availability of heavy logistic support in place at Epernay and already at the disposal of the 8e RH for the EBR's evaluation. Eventually 25 AMX13s were received by the 8e RH including FL11 turreted and Series 1 vehicles. The *2e Régiment de Dragons* were the first to evaluate the AMX13 in North Africa in regimental strength however. See www.amicale-8-hussards.com Also see the late Lt-Col Claude Aicardi's site *Cavaliers Blindés:*

http://cavaliers.blindes.free.fr for an understanding of how the wartime divisional structures still existed on paper at this time.

13. The 13e RDP employed the AMX13 squadron until 1955 when they re-equipped with wheeled vehicles. We thank Messieurs Jean-Pierre Benaut and Alain Bernard for their help in researching the 5e RH's early use of the AMX13. Monsieur Bernard is the son of the 5e RH's commanding officer at the time the first AMX13s were received and he later served as a Mle 51 crewman in the R.C.C.P (*Régiment Colonial de Chasseurs de Chars*) at Friedrichshaven. By 1955 the *3e Régiment de Spahis Algériens* and the 5e RH (both based in neighbouring encampments at Fritzlar) were completely equipped with the AMX13. The website of the *Amicale du 5e Regiment de Hussards'* includes a range of photos showing the first AMX13s deployed by the regiment in Fritzlar. While the EBR was regarded as a more suitable reconnaissance vehicle by the light cavalry regiments, the AMX13 was used in reconnaissance regiments in other armies, notably the Netherlands KL. Also see the late Lt-Col Claude Aicardi's site *Cavaliers Blindés*: http://cavaliers.blindes.free.fr/rgtdissous/5hussardsh.html

14. See Windrow, M. and Lyles., K. *French Foreign Legion Paratroops*. Osprey Elite. Osprey Publishing, UK. 1985.

15. See the late Lt-Col Claude Aicardi's extremely comprehensive website *Cavaliers Blindés*, which gives a full breakdown of the ABC regiments sent to Algeria as well as an orbat for the *Régiment Blindé Type AFN*. http://cavaliers.blindes.free.fr/gu/alg-rgt.html

16. See Molinié, Joseph. *Les Engins Blindés du Monde 1917-1967*, Argout-Editions, Paris, 1981. IGA Molinié noted that one of the significant reasons why the FL11 turret was an ideal requirement for the AMX13 in Indochina was its ability to employ American 75mm ammunition already available in quantity for the M24 and M4 tanks that equipped the French Army in that theater. At least 12 vehicles are believed to have been produced.

17. See p.52, *Document technique AMX 13 tonnes – 75 modele 51, châssis (texte)*, Saumur, 1963.

18. See p.69 Marest, Michel et Tauzin Michel. *L'Armement de Gros Calibre*. COMHART Tome 9. DGA. France. 2008. From the earliest design stages of the 12-ton tank's design in 1947, the *État Major de l'Armée de Terre* (EMAT) had requested an optical rangefinder as part of the fire control system, a wish that was never fulfilled. The tactic of firing from the halt was consequently taught from the very earliest days of the AMX13's service in the French Army. Only the most recent upgrades of the FL turrets were a solution provided in the form of laser rangefinding equipment.

19. See p.5-8. *Le Peloton d'AMX*. N.133. École d'Application de l'Arme Blindée et de la Cavalerie. Saumur, November 1960. As we shall see, the AMX13 SS11 was not available in the Patton regiments nor in the *Régiment de Chars Légers* until 1964 due to the very slow process of picking the preferred means of delivery for the SS11 missile in the *Arme Blindée Cavalerie* and the constant funding shortfalls resulting from the war in Algeria and its aftermath.

20. See the late Lt-Col Claude Aicardi's site *Cavaliers Blindés*: http://cavaliers.blindes.free.fr for a more complete understanding of how the postwar divisional structures described in this work were organized. Aicardi's research is detailed and comprehensive but knowledge of French is necessary to get full benefit of the site. Sadly no comparable English sources exist.

21. See Touzin, P. Les *véhicules blindés Français 1945-1977*. Editions EPA, France 1978. The SS11's arrival in the Arme Blindée Cavalerie came some 5 years after the basic tactical units for its employment had been prepared. The SS11 was not the only antitank missile tested on the AMX13 platform, and the VTT Mle 56 was marketed as a tank hunter with ENTAC missiles in the 1960s, an option selected for the Belgian Army. Other missile types eventually tested from AMX13 series vehicles are believed to include the HOT and Roland. The modifications necessary for the installation of the SS11 and the TCM fire control system onto the type D turret was described in the 1961 technical manual entitled: *MAT 6436/1, Guide Technique Sommaire de l'Equipement d'Engins Téléguidés Antichar SS. 11 monte sur char 13 t - 75 – mle 51 a tourelle FL. 10 D.*

22. See Touzin, P. Les *véhicules blindés Français 1945-1977*. Editions EPA, France 1978. Pierre Touzin notes a third gun as a possible weapon for the *revalorization* of the French AMX13 fleet: the 105mm gun then under development for the ERAC (*Engin de Reconnaissance à Chenilles*) in 1962 to replace the EBR. This weapon fired hollow charge rounds at a velocity of 1000 m/s with a lower chamber pressure than the CN 105 F1 that armed the AMX30B. It survived the cancellation of the ERAC and later emerged after much development (via the MECA/EFAB project) as the 105mm gun that armed the AMX10RC, designated CN 105 F3. It was later provided with APFSDS ammunition. He notes that the CN 90 F3 was extensively tested from September 1964 to November 1966 at Bourges.

23. See p.137 Marest, Michel et Tauzin Michel. *L'Armement de Gros Calibre*. COMHART Tome 9. DGA. France. 2008. Two earlier considerations for upgrading the Mle 51 were examined in 1962-63 by the EMAT and DGA and were undertaken at length by DEFA. These included the conversion of the AMX13 Mle 51 to Mle 58 standard by fitting the D1504 105mm gun into a modified FL10 turret (rebuilt to FL12 standard) and adopting the Obus-G round, or by developing a new 75/54/40 armour-piercing sub-calibre round for the existing CN 75 50 gun. The 75mm sub-calibre round was fired at a velocity of 1310 m/s. Both of these programmes were discarded due to the expected cost in comparison to converting the CN 75 50 to the D960 90mm configuration and due to the commonality of 90mm ammunition with the AML and upgraded EBR. The AMX13 armed with a 90mm gun was long envisioned as an alternate to the 105mm gunned Mle 58. An AMX13 armed with a Cn 90mm gun is mentioned in a provisional chassis spare parts list as early as September 1960 as the 'CHAR 13t-90-F1'. The photos show a 90mm armed tank equipped with infra-red equipment, some 6 or 7 years before funding was made available for series conversion and before the CN-90-F3 was perfected in 1964. The 90mm D960 gun underwent a slightly longer development than the similar D924 90mm upgrade performed on the EBR's lower

velocity 75 SA 49 gun because the higher velocity inherent to the longer gun fitted to the FL10 turret imparted a longer range. Accuracy at maximum range was initially an issue with the lighter 90mm round fired from the D960 but when it was standardized as the CN 90 F3 in 1966 the accuracy issues had been resolved.

24. See p.78 Marest, Michel et Tauzin Michel. *L'Armement de Gros Calibre*. COMHART Tome 9. DGA. France. 2008.

25. See Journal Officiel de l'Assemblée National No. 66. 1966: ministre des armées, Pierre Messmer. The slow production of the AMX30B and the delay and cancellation of the ERAC reconnaissance vehicle also added to the importance of the AMX13 C90 option. Also see Mortal, Patrick. *Les Armuriers de l'Etat, du Grand Siècle à la Globalisation, 1665-1989*, Villeneuve d'Ascq, Presses Universitaires du Septentrion. France, 2007. As an aside, Mortal stresses the importance in the latter part of the Cold War of the various rebuild programmes associated to armoured vehicles in the profitability of the state arsenals. This was of extreme importance in keeping the arsenals in work as the nuclear programme diverted credits away from conventional programmes. This must be considered in the decisions to rebuild the Mle 51s and EBRs with 90mm guns instead of buying the ERAC and Mle 58, and in the long delays in artillery and infantry weapons programs. Infra-red driving and gunnery equipment were to be retrofitted to existing AMX13 Mle 51s per the n. 5147 EMAT/3/ARMET order from the EMAT as of 27 July 1964. Technical instructions for the refit program followed in the manual MAT 6783/2 the first edition of which also appeared in 1964.

26. See Journal Officiel de l'Assemblée National No. 66. 1966: ministre des armées, Pierre Messmer. The 1967 divisional system required 5 divisions; 3 divisions for the defence of northeastern France (1e Corps d'Armée) and 2 more for the *Forces Francaises en Allemagne* (2e Corps d'Armée). Each of these divisions was expected to incorporate two mechanized brigades and a single motorized brigade. A sixth division stationed in south-west France was composed of two airborne brigades and one air portable brigade. The AMX30B and the rebuilt AMX13 C90 were of primal importance in the 1967 divisions, as was the purchase of the AM F3 155mm gun. The hard task of juggling the priority of these acquisitions on the 1966-76 budgets is confirmed by the equipment of some units being scaled back, particularly as some infantry regiments remained motorized. The adoption of the Division 1977 (of much simpler structure) was the most obvious consequence.

27. See p.71 Marest, Michel et Tauzin Michel. *L'Armement de Gros Calibre*. COMHART Tome 9. DGA. France. 2008, and *Notice descriptive de la famille 13 tonnes AMX*, DEFA, France 1965. The OB 105 AU Mle 50 had a fully enclosed casemate but its roof incorporated a cutout for its sighting equipment which reduced its protection from overhead airbursts appreciably. For direct fire the OB 105 Mle 50 AU's original direct fire sights were carried over to the self-propelled gun as standard equipment and 2 OCC hollow charge rounds for antitank use. Subsequent modification to the gun for export resulted in the gun's elevation movement changing to -4°30 to +70° and azimuth movement to +20°, a decrease in crew to 5 men and to the increase in stowage to 56 rounds (including 6 OCC antitank rounds) along with other minor changes. The construction of 160 of the OB 150 AU Mle 50 production vehicles at the ARE is documented on p.211. Barras. M. *L'Histoire de l'Arsenal de Roanne*. Editions Lyonnaises d'Art et d'Histoire. France, 1996.

28. See p.67 and p.121 Marest, Michel et Tauzin Michel. *L'Armement de Gros Calibre*. COMHART Tome 9. DGA. France. 2008. The turreted 105mm automoteur was sometimes referred to as the Mk.62 in unofficial English language sources, which may indicate that it was designated by DEFA or its successors as the OB 105 AU Mle 62 or similar, although this is not confirmed. It may also be possible that the later pattern export version of the fixed casemate OB 105 Mle 50 AU could have carried a designation similar to this for internal DEFA use, ie OB 105 Mle 61 AU.

29. Sample of the variations in official designations for the Char de Dépannage. Some of the variation was likely due to the fact that it was used in multiple combat arms.

Char de dépannage AMX	Reserve de cavalerie (1958/59)
Char AMX de dépannage	Ecole d'application de l'Arme blindée et la cavalerie (1963)
Char de dépannage	DEFA (1965)
Char de dépannage AMX M. 55 L'AMX de dépannage	Ecole supérieure et d'application du matériel
Char de dépannage AMX Mle 55	Touzin, Pierre. Les Véhicules Blindés Français 1945-1977, Éditions E.P.A, France 1978.

30. A similar state of affairs existed with the Poseur de Pont, although it was only employed in the divisional engineers' regiments and the variation is not easily explained.

L'AMX poseur de pont	Ecole d'application de l'Arme blindée et la cavalerie (1963)
Char léger poseur de pont Poseur de pont	DEFA (1965)
Char AMX 13 poseur de pont	Ecole supérieure et d'application du matériel
Char AMX poseur de pont	Ministère des Armées MAT-3247, Guide d'entretien du char AMX poseur de pont

Additionally, the designation *AMX Poseur de Pont Mle 57* is also used in some documents, and the F1 designation (or F1 bis) may actually refer to the bridge. See p.57-59. Brindeau, P. et Mallet, M. *Materiels du Genie*. COMHART Tome 7. DGA. France. 1996.

31. See p.165-166. R. M. Ogorkiewicz, *Design and Development of Fighting Vehicles*, Doubleday & Company Inc, 1968. The characteristics of the VTT Mle 56 are outlined in the following sources: p.284-286. *Le Transport de Troupe Chenillé Modèle 1956 AMX 13*, p.33, *Les Chars Francais du Musée des Blindés*, Catalogue 1, Centre de Documentation sur les Engins Blindés (CDEB) et de Association des Amis du Musée des Blindés (AAMB), Saumur, France, and p.53, *AMX – 13 tonnes – 75 – Modèle 51, Documentation Technique – Chassis (Texte)*, Ecole d'Application de l'Arme Blindée et de la Cavalerie, Saumur, June 1963. Touzin notes that the VTT Mle 56 or a similar vehicle based on the AMX13 might have entered service a decade earlier, were it not for the infantry's indecision regarding the size of the embarked infantry group and the consequent evaluation of competing designs from Hotchkiss and Batignoles-Chatillon. See p.91-108. Pierre Touzin, *Les véhicules blindés français 1945-1977*, Éditions E.P.A, France. 1978. Production of 661 VTT Mle 56s at ARE is documented on p.212. Barras. M. *L'Histoire de l'Arsenal de Roanne*. Editions Lyonnaises d'Art et d'Histoire. France, 1996., although production was also undertaken at FCM and at Creusot-Loire.

32. The first production series of VTT Mle 56 received the CAFL 38 (Compagnie des Ateliers et Forges de la Loire) turret armed with the 7.5mm MAC31 Machinegun. Later vehicles were equipped with the 12.5mm mounting. The 20mm F1 cannon armed turret replaced both in later years. The CN 20 F1 was based on the DEFA 20.693 20mm cannon and was intended for use against ground targets or helicopters. The T20-13 20mm turret fitted to the VTT was developed at the MAS (Manufacture Nationale d'Armes de Saint-Etienne) arsenal at St Etienne as the TOUCAN 1 whereas the TH20 TOUCAN 2 had a 2-man crew and image intensification sights for use at night, and was destined for the more sophisticated AMX10P. See p.54. Lesavre, René et de Launet, Michel. *Les Armements de Défense Anti-Aérienne par Canons et Armes Automatiques*, COMHART Volume 8/3, DGA, France 2007.

33. See p.112-114. Brindeau, P. et Mallet, M. *Materiels du Génie*. COMHART Tome 7. DGA. France. 1996. Only 46 VTT Mle 56 Cargo were delivered to the French army.

34. See p.174-177, Touzin, Pierre. *Les Véhicules Blindés Français 1945-1977*, Éditions E.P.A, France, 1978. The plan to replace the M40 and M41 in French service was seriously delayed by extensive efforts in the mid-1950s to test out a turreted 155mm self-propelled gun built by the Lorraine company. DEFA conducted its own design study of the AMX13 chassis to mount a 155mm gun in a far simpler medium artillery weapon in 1958. The 155mm gun was designed by the Atelier de Bourges on the basis of the towed OB-155-50 155mm howitzer adopted in 1950. The prototype mounting on an AMX13 chassis was built in 1959. In 1962 the second prototype was built and a 10 vehicle *préserie* was ordered. Different 155mm howitzer and gun configurations were tested and several muzzle brake types were evaluated in order to deal with the problem of recoil on the light chassis. In spring 1965 the 155mm gun was standardized with the lengthened barrel as the CN 155 F3. The self-propelled gun was designated *Canon de 155mm Modèle F3 Automouvant* or CN 155 F3 AM. The *Section Technique de l'Armée* extensively tested the 10 pre-production vehicles in 1966. Production was initiated in September 1966. In August 1966 unit trials were undertaken with the *74e Regiment d'Artillerie*. Production vehicles began delivery to the French Army in July 1968, to the 74e RA and the 1e RAMa. Also see p.184-187. Marest, Michel et Tauzin Michel. *L'Armement de Gros Calibre*. COMHART Tome 9. DGA. France. 2008. This text gives slightly different dates for the prototype testing and production order from the Touzin text. Once the Division 1977 was put in place the army conducted biannual divisional maneuvers every 2 years. These maneuvers were conducted over vast expanses of countryside to test out the logistic and communications capability as well as the fighting capability of the 4 *régiments de mêlés* (the 2 armoured and 2 mechanized infantry units) that formed the "teeth" of the division. One of the problems that became evident quickly was that artillery units with only 3 AM F3 batteries were ill suited to supporting divisions composed of 4 regiments. The solution decided in 1980 was to create a fourth battery in each artillery regiment, which was simplified by the arrival of the Au F1 self-propelled gun to replace the AM F3 in divisional artillery units, a process that began around 1981. The post 1981 divisional artillery regiments equipped with the AM F3 included 4 batteries of 5 guns as shown in the Division 1977 chart. Our thanks to Lt-Col Denis Verdier, former commander of the *4e Batterie, 1e Régiment d'Artillerie*, for his assistance in researching the AM F3 in the Division 1977.

35. See p.191-196 Robineau. *Relations Internationales*. The contract No F37MWPA57 "*Relatif à l'Étude d'une Tourelle de Char Armée du Canon Bitube Antiaérien de 30mm*" dated March 29th 1957 is reproduced verbatim.

36. See p.193-195. Touzin, Pierre. *Les Véhicules Blindés Français 1945-1977*, Éditions E.P.A, France 1978. Touzin notes the interest of the Swiss in this vehicle and that a production SAMM 400 turret was loaned to Switzerland in 1967; it is not recorded if it was radar-equipped.

37. See p.37-38 and p.43-45. Lesavre, René et de Launet, Michel. *Les Armements de Défense Anti-Aérienne par Canons et Armes Automatiques*, COMHART Volume 8/3, DGA, France 2007. The HS 30mm cannon was already in order in a single mounting towed canon for the French artillery that began to be delivered in 1960. This text explains that even with the slightly heavier hull the SAMM 400(A) turret mounted on the 30mm Bitube DCA was overweight at 17.8 tonnes (and top heavy) and was better suited to the AMX30 hull tested out as early as 1965.

38. The AMX13 tested in Sweden was French *immatriculation* 608 0450 but carried Swedish Registration 80 308 and Swedish national insignia throughout its testing. Partly because of its longer ranged gun and better protection, and its thicker armour better protecting its crew against radiation, the Swedes purchased the Centurion instead of the AMX13. The AMX13 concept and the FL10 turret were both very influential in the development of the S-Tank

concept, however, and one of the evaluating officers of the 1952 AMX13 trials in Sweden was Sven Berge. The nature of American interest in the AMX13 after 1952 is debatable; and it should neither be overestimated nor dismissed. American interest in the AMX13 around 1960 is noted on p.45 Robineau. *Relations Internationales* and in the Barras text. These texts describe US interest around 1960 in the FL11 turreted AMX13 but do not specify if this was to serve as a template for their own design for a light air portable tank, or if they were contemplating purchasing examples. See p.49. *Foreign Relations of the United States, 1964-1968, Volume XII, Western Europe. Memorandum from the President's Special Assistant for National Security Affairs (Bundy) to Secretary of Defense McNamara. Department of State, United States of America. Washington April 8, 1964*. This memo written by McGeorge Bundy describes General Billotte's mission to the United States with official sanction from De Gaulle to address the matter of US license production of the AMX13 and AMX30 at the highest levels (and, notably, without the presence of the ambassador). American licence production of the AMX13 was proposed by the French along with the US Army's adoption of the AMX30 tank. The American response is not recorded but no production in the USA ever ensued.

39. See P.113-114. Robineau, Bertrand. *Relations Internationales*. COMHART Tome 5. DGA. France. 2003., and see 2e séance du 4 December 1951. Swiss National Assembly Proceedings of December 1951. The Swiss general staff's study of the Arnhem operation and other paratroop attacks during the Second World War left them particularly fearful of airborne assaults in the event of war because Switzerland's mechanized forces were relatively small and the army's equipment was obsolete. Swiss acquisitions and aims are also described in CN 17. séance du 05.10.1960. Swiss National Assembly Proceedings of May 1960. Please also see the following website for further information on the Swiss L PZ 51: http://militaerfahrzeuge.ch/ with thanks to Christoph Zimmerli. For details of the turreted *AMX 105mm Obusier Automoteur à Casemate Tournante* see p.7. SOGAFLASH 2013, Schweizerische Offiziersgesellschaft der Artillerie, Ausgabe Nr. 23, Juli 2013, Switzerland, 2013. This weapon, developed in France in 1958, was tested at troop level in Switzerland in March 1963. The Swiss artillery followed with requests for 33 detail design changes in late 1962 for production vehicles intending the turreted 105mm self-propelled gun to be adopted as standard equipment. This version of the OB 105 AU (sometimes referred to as the OB 105 AU Mk.62 in existing literature) employed a 30 calibre gun with a range of nearly 18 km. It was subsequently dropped from consideration as the Swiss Artillery's standard SPG when the Swiss Army decided to adopt the more powerful 155mm calibre gun. The US M109 entered service in Switzerland in 1968.

40. The impact of the AMX13 on the future S-Tank is documented in Ogorkiewicz, Robert. *S Tank*. AFV Weapons Profile 38. Profile Publications. Windsor, U.K. 1971. Swedish evaluation reports of the AMX13 in 1952 were translated into French and informed several modifications to the AMX13 design. See Arnell, S. *Considerations Préliminaires sur les Expériences de Tirs Faites Avec le Char AMX13 et Propositions pour Certaines Ameliorations*. 18.06.1952. (translation from the Swedish for DEFA), Berge, S. *Remarques Théoriques Concernant le Char AMX 75 m.51* (sic). (translation from the Swedish for DEFA), Carougeau, IGA. *Rapport sur les Essais Effectués en Suède avec le Char AMX, 13 tonnes. Periode du 24/3 au 9/7 1952*. St Cloud. 7/6/1952. -all of which are contained in SE/KrA/0062/D/01/016:H/F 1 in the Swedish Archives, documentation carefully translated into French and including reports by Sven Berge and comments from IGA Carougeau and IGA Roland. See P.58 and p.75. Robineau, Bertrand. *Relations Internationales*. COMHART Tome 5. DGA. France. 2003. There was a significant amount of coyness on the West Germans part regarding their intentions to buy French weaponry, equalled only by French wishful thinking in their conviction that such a purchase was inevitable. West Germany's true intentions to rebuild their own arms industry were not perceived by the French until about 1960. These were subsequently borne out by the saga of the Europa Panzer, which resulted in the AMX30 and the Leopard 1- and West German domination of the continental European NATO MBT market by the 1970s.

41. See Urrisk, R.M. Brigadier Mag. Bundesheer Truppendienst Ausgabe 1/2005 Waffengattungen des Osterreichischen Bundesheeres. Vienna. 2005.

42. See P.58 and p.75. Robineau, Bertrand. *Relations Internationales*. COMHART Tome 5. DGA. France. 2003. The official Italian designation for the VTT Mle 56 was based on its number of embarked infantry: *Veicolo Trasporto Truppa e da Combattimento, VTC AMX.12*. See p.589-592. "AMX-13 e Derivati", Storia dei Mezzi Corazzati, No. 74, Fratelli Fabbri Editori, 1976. Also see *Veicolo Trasporto Truppa e da Combattimento, VTC AMX.12*. MAT3535 di 1960/CM7 7803. Catalogo delle Parti di Ricambio ed Equipaggiamento. Edizione 1969. Ministero della Difesa.

43. See p.102 Robineau, Bertrand. *Relations Internationales*. COMHART Tome 5. DGA. France. 2003.

44. Van den Heuvel, P. en Staarman, A. AMX voertuigen in de Koninklijke Landmacht 1961-1983.

45. See Van den Heuvel, P. en Staarman, A. AMX voertuigen in de Koninklijke Landmacht 1961-1983. The Dutch Army did its own tests with the AMX13 Mle 56 VTT in 1960 which revealed mixed results. The KL had already closely followed the West German tests of the Mle 56 VTT conducted in 1957-58. The *Bundeswehr* would have (for political reasons and purpose of Franco-German cooperation) purchased a French product, but they concluded that the AMX Mle 56 VTT did not meet the *Bundeswehr*'s requirements. A summary of the German report was annexed to the more favourable Dutch field test report and was considered in the Dutch decision to buy the Mle 56 VTT. The German report criticised AMX Mle 56 VTT as not mobile enough, insufficiently armed and obsolescent mechanically. The harsh German judgement was directed specifically at the VTT. These same issues were seemingly accepted (possibly for political reasons) by the Dutch *faute de mieux*. The KL's Deputy Chief of Staff Lieutenant General A. V. Van den Wall Bake described the Mle 56 VTT as a fairly reliable and tactically acceptable armoured personnel carrier that met the KL's needs. See 1TH9-230B. *Technische Handleiding. Gevechtsvoertuig, Pantser, Rups, Infanterie: Type 2D (AMX) en afgeleide typen. Bediening en Gebruikersonderhoud*, Koninklijke Landmacht. Netherlands. 1967. The KL infantry teams that employed the

PRI were issued a wide range of weaponry different from that stowed in a French Army VTT Mle 56. Stowage for FN FAL rifles, an MAG 58 GPMG, M72 LAW antitank rockets and an 84mm rocket launcher with 24 rounds were carried as standard for the embarked infantry squad. Another source which illustrates the KL's modernization in the 1950s and 1960s is Ruys, Sander. *De Centuriontank in Nederlandse Dienst*, Armamentaria 2002. Legermuseum, Delft. Netherlands, 2002. Although specifically written with regard to the Centurion it explains how the KL's armoured force evolved and the strategic planning that lay behind the creation of reconnaissance and armoured units in the 1950s and 1960s.

46. Dutch language sources criticize the availability of the PRA towards the end of its service, a problem also encountered with the Dutch Centurion fleet, and very likely linked to vehicle age, an inadequate stock of spares and mileage restrictions, especially for units based in the Netherlands. See Van den Heuvel, P. en Staarman, A. *AMX voertuigen in de Koninklijke Landmacht 1961-1983*.

47. See p. 115 Robineau, Bertrand. *Relations Internationales*. COMHART Tome 5. DGA. France. 2003.

48. See p. 55-74. Levey, Zach, *Israel and the Western Powers, 1952-1960*, ISBN 0-8078-2368-6, The University of North Carolina Press, USA. 1997.

49. See p.103 Goodarzi, Jubin M. *Syria and Iran: Diplomatic Alliance and Power Politics in the Middle East*, I.B. Tauris & Co Ltd, 2009 and p.199. Cordesman, Anthony H. *The Military Balance in the Middle East*, Center for Strategic and International Studies, 2004. Also see Assad, Moustafa. *AMX13 in Lebanon*. Blue Steel Series No.5. Canada. 2016. This photographic book tells the story of the AMX13 in Lebanese service and is the most up to date treatment of the subject. Interestingly, while the first two purchases of AMX13 Mle 51 and Mle 58s were repainted locally prior to issue in the Lebanese Army brigades, the batch of AMX13 C90s purchased in 1984 retained their French liveries for some time.

50. See p.121. Robineau, Bertrand. *Relations Internationales*. COMHART Tome 5. DGA. France. 2003. Qatar was a market long coveted by the French, who deferred for most of the 1960s to British influence in the small gulf nation. This certainly impacted French chances to sell the Mle 51 in the area. French sales of arms to Qatar followed in the 1970s.

51. See p.116. Robineau, Bertrand. *Relations Internationales*. COMHART Tome 5. DGA. France. 2003.

52. See p.386. Kolodziej, Edward A. *Making and Marketing Arms – The French Experience and Its Implications for the International* System, Princeton University Press, ISBN 0-691-07734-7.

53. See p.45-48. Fogliani, Ricardo Sigal. *Blindados Argentinos de Uruguay y Paraguay*. Ayer y Hoy, Argentina. 1997. The task of performing the 1979 modernization of the Argentinian AMX13 Mle 58 was given to two companies: Klockner-Humboldt-Deutz of Germany and TENSA (*Talleres Electrometalurgicos Norte Sociedad Anonima*), an Argentinian engineering company with extensive experience in manufacturing automotive, aerospace and heavy engineering equipment. TENSA had already established a military engineering division headed by one of the country's best defense engineers, Salvador Porto. The adoption of the Deutz diesel was accompanied by other modifications performed by TENSA to the Mle 58's FL12 turrets, including the replacement of the coaxial MAC31 with the MAG 58 7.62mm machine gun (with a second MAG mounted on the commander's cupola), infrared gunnery sights, and American VCR-3200-2W radio equipment. The driver was also provided with infrared driving lights.

54. Libro Blanco de la Defensa 2010. Ministerio de Defensa Argentino. 2010. and see p.45-48. Fogliani, Ricardo Sigal. *Blindados Argentinos de Uruguay y Paraguay*. Ayer y Hoy, Argentina. 1997.

55. The Ecuadorian Army has an excellent website www.cehist.mil.ec with many accessible official publications regarding the army and its campaigns. See p.106-118. Espinoza (Ed.). *Historias y Tradiciones Militares del Ejercito Ecuatoriano*. CEHE. Quito, Ecuador.2011. and see p.122-143. Nunez, E.C. *Brief History of the Army of Ecuador*. CEHE. Quito, Ecuador.2014. An image of one of the Ecuadorean Mle 58s being prepared for conversion to the new engine and fire controls in the hangars at the Companya de Apoyo Logistico No.11 is on p. 140 in Nunez, E.M. *Logistica Poder de Combate: Historia de los Servicios en el Ecuador*. Centro des Estudios Historicos del Ejercito No.31. CEHE, Quito, Ecuador. 2014. The authors additionally thank General Jorge Andrade Piedra Montenegro, a long serving Ecuadorean armoured cavalryman, the former commander of the Galapagos Brigade and military historian, for his kind help and for the use of his photographs in this work.

56. See Familia Acorazada del Ejercito de Chile – Historia de los Vehiculos Blindados del Ejercito (1936-2009), Impreso en los Talleres del Instituto Geográfico Militar, Ejercito de Chile. Also see p.386, Kolodziej, Edward, A. *Making and Marketing Arms – The French Experience and Its Implications for the International* System, Princeton University Press. USA. 1987.

57. The chart below illustrates the range of Creusot-Loire AMX13 vehicles offered in the late 1970s. The AMX PP and the AMX CD Mle 55 were both available as built to order vehicles assembled at AMX. (Source Creusot-Loire)

Creusot-Loire Designation	English Designation	Remark
le système d'artillerie de 155 mm sur AMX 13	The 155-mm artillery system mounted on AMX 13	The system consisted of 3 types of AMX 13-based vehicles
AMX 13 – 155 mm Mle F3 automouvant	AMX 13 self-propelled gun model F3	The 155mm gun.
AMX 13 – VTT/VCA (Véhicule Chenillé d'Accompagnement d'artillerie	AMX 13 – APC/VCA (Tracked accompanying vehicle)	The support vehicle which carries the gun crew and ammunition. It is designed for towing an ammunition trailer.

Creusot-Loire Designation	English Designation	Remark
AMX 13 – VTT/LT (Véhicule Lieutenant de Tir)	AMX 13 – APC/LT (Battery executive Command Post Vehicle)	The fire control vehicle which is used by battery commander.
La famille AMX 13 – VTT (Véhicule Transport de Troupe)	AMX 13 – APC family (Armoured Personnel Carrier)	
AMX 13 – VTT/VCI (Véhicule de Combat d'Infanterie)	AMX 13 – APC/VCI (Infantry Combat Vehicle)	The basic VTT Mle 56 which could be supplied with the CAFL 38 turret or S470 cupola.
AMX 13 – VTT/PC (Véhicule de Commandement)	AMX 13 – APC/PC (Command Post Vehicle)	
AMX 13 – VTT/TB (Véhicule Transport de Blessés)	AMX 13 – APC/TB (Ambulance Vehicle)	Armoured Ambulance for 4 stretcher cases.
AMX 13 – VTT/PM (Véhicule Porte-Mortier)	AMX 13 – APC/PM (Mortar Vehicle)	For 81mm mortar.
AMX 13 – VTT/RATC (Radar de Tir pour Artillerie de Campagne)	AMX 13 – APC/RATAC (RATAC vehicle)	RATAC is the French abbreviation for Field Artillery Fire Control Radar.
AMX 13 – VTT/VCA (Véhicule Chenillé d'Accompagnement d'artillerie	AMX 13 – APC/VCA (Tracked accompanying vehicle)	Artillery Support vehicle.
AMX 13 – VTT/LT (Véhicule Lieutenant de Tir)	AMX 13 – APC/LT (Battery executive Command Post Vehicle)	Battery Command Vehicle.
le char AMX 13 à canon de 105 mm	The AMX 13 tank mounted with a 105-mm gun	AMX13 Mle 58.
AMX 13 – VCG (Véhicule de Combat du Génie)	AMX 13 – VCG (Engineer Combat Vehicle)	Based on the VTT Mle 56 with dozer and fitted for towing a trailer.
AMX13 – anti-aérien bitube de 20 mm	AMX13 – air defence 20 mm twin-barreled gun	The AMX13 mounted with the TA20/RA20S turret for use as a short-range air defence weapon system.

58. See Annual Budget Statement, Parliament of Singapore, 12 March 1968, see *Giving Strength to Our Nation – The SAF and Its People*. Singapore Ministry of Defence, 2015. And see p.385; Lee Kuan Yew, *From Third World to First: The Singapore Story, 1965-2000*, Volume 2, Singapore, 2000.

59. See Annual budget statement, Parliament of Singapore, 12 March 1968 regarding SAF training in Israel and see p.39, *The Black Berets – Training Transformation in Action*, Armour Training Institute, Singapore, 2006. Regarding the Limited Depot Overhaul.

60. See Yap, Matthew. "SAF tanks upgraded locally", The Straits Times, 8 July 1988; Mickey Chiang, "Fighting Fit – The Singapore Armed Forces", Times Editions, 1990, also see p. 170-171; Ministry of Defence, Army News, Issue No. 164, Mar / April 2009.

61. See p.9. ST Engineering, "New Lease of Life for the SM1 SLEP", Sunburst Alpha, Issue Jan-Mar 2008, Ministry of Defence, Army News, Issue No. 164, Mar / April 2009.

62. See: Ministry of Defence, Factsheet – 328 Singapore Combat Engineers. Retrieved on 25 September 2016, from: https://www.mindef.gov.sg/imindef/press_room/official_releases/nr/2004/jun/30jun04_nr/30jun04_fs5.html (for details of the SLB).

63. Source: PUSAT KESENJATAAN KAVALERI or Pussenkav TNI-AD (Army Cavalry Weapons Center).

64. See Gérard Turbé, *An Original Solution to AMX-13 Modernisation*, International Defense Review 8/1989.

65. *Defensa Nacional Carro de Combate 1*.

66. See pg. 165, Jane's Armour & Artillery 1997-98 and p. 16-17, Br. Balzan Yamilet and Br. Flores Frankenry, *SISTEMA DE INFORMACIÓN GERENCIAL PARA LA ADMINISTRACIÓN DE LOSI ESPEDIENTES MILITARES DE LA UNIDAD DE APOYO 103 GAC/LCM "G/J. JOSE GREGORIO MONAGAS"*, Universidad Rafael Urdaneta, Facultad de Ingeniería, Escuela de Computación, Maracaibo, Edo. Zulia, Republica Bolivariana de Venezuela, Noviembre 2002.

67. See José Lugo Marin, *Fénix y Ráfaga*, http://www.fav-club.com/2014/01/21/fenix-y-rafaga/ (retrieved 22 July 2016), also see Gonzalo Jiménez Mora, "El vehiculo blindado AMX-13M56 VCI del Ejército Bolivariano", http://www.fav-club.com/2015/12/12/el-vehiculo-blindado-amx-13m56-vci-del-ejercito-bolivariano-2/ , and R Barrett Edwards, *VENEZUELA ALLOCATES $19 MILLION FOR AMX-13 TANK UPGRADE*, Forecast international – International Military Market (www.forecastinternational), 19 February 2014, FAV-Club (www.fav-club.com) with press information from Bolivarian Army, Army Recognition (www.armyrecognition.com), Defence & Security News, *Army of Venezuela to modernize French-made AMX-13 APC with Russian-made turret MB2-04*, 22 February 2014. and *Gaceta Oficial de la República Bolivariana de Venezuela*, Número 40.352, Caracas, lunes 10 de febrero de 2014.

68. See pg. 165, Jane's Armour & Artillery 1997-98 and CRNL. EMC. Carlos Procel S., *La Evolucion Cientifica y Tecnologica de la Fuerza Terrestre y su Influencia en la Seguridad Nacional*. Republica del Ecuador Secretaria General del Consejo de Seguridad Nacional Instituto de Altos Estudios Nacionales, XXVIII Curso 2000-2001. Quito 2001.

69. See Alejo Marchessini, *El AMX-13 "Alacrán" fracasa en Perú en sus pruebas de tiro*, Defensa.com, Edefa Group S.A., 16 November 2011.(http://defensa.com/index.php?option=...ica&Itemid=163)

70. See ARC Web articles *"AMX13 Retrofit Pindad itu Mulai Berjalan"* (http://arc.web.id/berita/619-a,x-13-retrofit-pindad-itu-mulai-berjalan dated 1 April 2014) and *"Blaar! Dan Tank Retrofit itu pun Mengaum"* (http://arc.web.id/artikel/623-blaar-dan-tank-retrofit-itu-pun-mengaum dated 14 April 2014) for information concerning the PINDAD mobility trials and the firing tests.

71. The author Guy Gibeau's recollection of experiences with the AMX13.

72. Theoretically, if ammunition was staged and unpacked prior to the AMX13 platoon moving to a *rendez-vous* point to reload, the automatic loading system was quickly replenished. In practice, as main armament ammunition was kept packed in wooden boxes and the MAC31 was provided with hand loaded drum magazines, replenishment took far longer than one would imagine.

73. Guy Gibeau could still recall many years later when one of his subordinate AMX13 SS11 tank commanders loaded high explosive rounds into an AMX13 SS11's *barillets* in defiance of recommended operating procedures during a range period in West Germany. The rammer slammed the high explosive round into the breech fouling the edge. The result was one 75mm high explosive round with the shell crushed back into the casing. Tense hours followed as the horrified crew and their officers removed the impacted round to a safe location for detonation, fearing every moment that the shell would detonate.

74. See p.8, *Cours par Correspondance des Officiers de Réserve de Cavalerie, Documentation Technique No. 3, Le Char de 13 tonnes Mle 51 (AMX)*, Cycle 1955 – 1956, Saumur, 1955.

75. Further recollection of his experiences with the AMX13 by Guy Gibeau. Accounts of the discomfort of the AMX13 are easily accumulated if one talks to other former crewmen (the authors thank Bernard Canonne amongst others). Many are the stories of gunners and commanders getting their boots caught in the oscillating turret joint. Discomfort increased if the crew members were above average height or if they were of a stocky or heavyset build, as was sometimes the case with commanders who were officers. Despite the lack of space tank suits with straps to ease extraction of injured crews were not issued until the early 1980s in France. Swedish comments on the AMX13 trials in 1952 noted that there was not adequate space for administering first aid to injured crew members.

76. See pg. 35, Maj Gen (Retd) A K Dewan, AVSM, VrC, *Reminiscences of 20 Lancers In the Battle of Chushul (Ladakh) – 18 & 19 November 1962*, Post Horn Gallop 57, Cavalry's Officers' Association, September 2013. A K Dewan had assumed command of the Chushul tank detachment a few days after the airlift as the Squadron Commander was evacuated due to altitude sickness.

77. See "While Memory is Fresh" by Maj Gen Jagjit Singh, Lancer Publishers & Distributors, New Delhi, 2006. Jagjit Singh was the brigade major of the 114 Brigade in 1962.

78. See Cloughley, Brian. "*A History of the Pakistan Army – Wars and Insurrections*", ISBN: 978-1-63144-038-0, Carrel Books, Skyhorse Publishing, 2016.

79. See Dunstan, Simon. "The Six Day War 1967 : Sinai", Osprey Publishing, 2009 also see p.17. Hofrichter Paul, "Red Armour – A history", Merriam Press, Military Monograph 163, Bennington, Vermont, 2012. and p.63 Gawrych, George W. "The Albatross of Decisive Victory: War and Policy Between Egypt and Israel in the 1967 and 1973 Arab-Israeli Wars", Greenwood Press, 2000.

80. See Brendan McNally, M50 Ontos: The Forgotten Tank-Killer, Defense Media Network, 12 February 2013 (http://www.defensemedianetwork.com/stories/m50ontostheforgottentankkiller/) and Sebastien Roblin, In 1965, U.S. and Dominican Tanks Fought Brief, Violent Skirmishes. https://warisboring.com/in1965usanddominicantanks foughtbriefviolentskirmishesf206040e66b3#.6j73xm8q9. While these are not primary sources, they feature some press photos taken at the period which show a Dominican L-60 and a burnt-out Dominican AMX-13 that were captured by the USMC.

81. See Grandolini, A. "Armor of the Vietnam War (2) Asian Forces", Concorde Publications, Hong Kong, 1998. Many thanks also to Ken Conboy and Darasy Var who made available many photos and much information about the Cambodian and Laotian armored forces. Also see p.13, Conboy and Bowra, The War in Cambodia 1970–75 (1989).